Discovering Fiction

A READER *of* AMERICAN SHORT STORIES

STUDENT'S BOOK 1

■ JUDITH KAY

■ ROSEMARY GELSHENEN

CAMBRIDGE
UNIVERSITY PRESS

PUBLISHED BY THE PRESS SYNDICATE OF THE UNIVERSITY OF CAMBRIDGE
The Pitt Building, Trumpington Street, Cambridge, United Kingdom

CAMBRIDGE UNIVERSITY PRESS
The Edinburgh Building, Cambridge CB2 2RU, UK
40 West 20th Street, New York, NY 10011–4211, USA
10 Stamford Road, Oakleigh, VIC 3166, Australia
Ruiz de Alarcón 13, 28014 Madrid, Spain
Dock House, The Waterfront, Cape Town 8001, South Africa

http://www.cambridge.org

First published 2001

Printed in the United States of America

Typeface Adobe Garamond   *System* QuarkXPress®   [AH]

A catalog record for this book is available from the British Library

Discovering fiction—student's book 1 : a reader of American short stories / [edited by] Judith Kay [and] Rosemary Gelshenen.
    p. cm.
    Includes bibliographical references and index.
    ISBN 0-521-00559-0 (pb.)
    1. English language–Textbooks for foreign speakers. 2. United States–Social life and customs–Fiction. 3. Short stories, American. I. Title: Discovering fiction–student's book one. II. Kay, Judith. III. Gelshenen, Rosemary.
    PE 1128 .D485 2001
    428.6'4.–dc21   00-065090

ISBN 0 521 00559 0 Student's Book 1
ISBN 0 521 00235 4 Instructor's Manual 1
ISBN 0 521 00351 2 Student's Book 2
ISBN 0 521 65448 3 Instructor's Manual 2

Art direction, book design, and layout services: Adventure House, NYC

Illustrations: Dan Brown: *Eleven, Two Thanksgiving Day Gentlemen, The Kiss;* Rosemary Fox: *The Fun They Had, The Tigress and Her Mate;* Miles Hyman: *The Blanket, The Mirror, Snake Dance, The Woman;* Lori Mitchell: *The Bracelet, Home;* Rick Powell: *A Secret for Two; You Go Your Way, I'll Go Mine;* Alexis Seabrook: *Johanna.*

See acknowledgments on page 214, which is an extension of this copyright page.

To our students, who have begun their journey in learning English. We hope this book will introduce you to the richness of American literature and that you will continue to read and explore.

About the Authors

JUDITH KAY has extensive experience teaching writing, communication skills, and grammar. She now teaches an academic composition class at Broward Community College in Broward County, Florida. Previously, she taught at Marymount Manhattan College in New York City, where she and Rosemary Gelshenen were colleagues. In addition, Kay has taught seminars in writing, and she and Gelshenen have collaborated on teaching curriculum and presented workshops at regional and international meetings of Teachers of English to Speakers of Other Languages (TESOL).

Kay has a master's degree in TESOL from Hunter College and is a member of Phi Beta Kappa. She has published both short stories and poetry.

ROSEMARY GELSHENEN teaches literature, creative writing, and grammar in New York City at both Marymount Manhattan College and New York University. Formerly, she taught English at Norman Thomas High School and was a teacher trainer for the New York City Board of Education. Her awards include the Veritas Medal for Excellence in Education (1986) and New York City Teacher of the Year (1983). She also received two Impact II grants for innovative methods of teaching.

Gelshenen's articles on teaching methods have appeared in numerous educational publications, and she lectures on literary topics. She is the author of *Instant English Literature* (1994), a lighthearted approach to the lives and works of nineteenth century English novelists.

Contents

Contents

To the Student

The fourteen stories in this book, by American authors of diverse backgrounds, present a variety of themes and styles. You will find these stories an exciting way to learn English. Each author represented here was influenced by his or her own ethnic background and life experience. As you read, think about ways in which your experiences and feelings are similar to or different from those presented in the stories.

In the classroom, you will find studying literature with this text an interesting way to improve your skills in reading and oral communication as well as your understanding of vocabulary and grammar. Of course, reading the work of good writers also enhances your writing skills.

As you enter the wonderful world of literature, you will meet people and go places you will never forget. Enjoy the journey.

JUDITH KAY
ROSEMARY GELSHENEN

To the Instructor

As teachers, we have seen many students eager to learn English but frustrated by the challenges of mastering the language. Some of our students' favorite lessons, however, are those in which they read and discuss short stories. In fact, students and teachers alike find that lessons incorporating short stories provide some of the most interesting ways to focus on reading skills, vocabulary, and even grammar.

An extra bonus in learning a language through literature is that stories are rooted in culture – in this case, that of America. The authors of the stories in this text represent different backgrounds and experiences in the rich heritage of the United States. As most teachers would agree, celebrating diversity promotes understanding and tolerance. Moreover, building our students' self-esteem should be a goal in every classroom.

We hope you enjoy the stories you are about to read. You are giving your students a special opportunity by guiding them through the new world of American literature.

JUDITH KAY
ROSEMARY GELSHENEN

Introduction

Discovering Fiction Student's Book 1 is an interactive, literature-based reading text for intermediate students of North American English. Through activities focused on authentic short stories by American writers, students develop their knowledge of vocabulary and grammar while improving their reading, oral communication, and writing skills.

The activities are carefully designed to encourage students' discovery of the ideas and meanings in the stories, giving students a sense of empowerment and control over their learning. For example, the text helps students master the skill of guessing meaning from context during a first reading. Students lacking this skill can become overly reliant on dictionaries, computers, or instructors for definitions. When students read without relying on such aids, they are often surprised at how much they already know and what they can figure out, which gives them increased confidence in their abilities.

Underlying *Discovering Fiction* is the philosophy that reading literature is an engaging way for students to learn a language. Students find stories especially motivating and naturally want to communicate their ideas about them. This text encourages pair work, small group work, and class discussion, giving students many opportunities to learn through interacting with others.

ORGANIZATION OF THE BOOK

Student's Book 1 is thematically organized into five parts. Each part consists of two or three chapters, with each chapter containing one short story and related activities. Since vocabulary and grammar activities in each chapter pertain only to the story being read, several options are possible for working through the book: (1) using the book sequentially from the first chapter to the last, (2) going through all the stories in a part but reading the parts out of sequence as appropriate, or (3) reading individual stories in any order the instructor desires. An advantage to reading all the stories in one part is that the instructor can then make use of the Summing Up section at the end of the part. The Summing Up sections allow students to compare the themes and ideas of the two or three preceding stories through discussion and writing; exercises to review idioms, expressions, and grammar are also included in Summing Up.

PRE-READING

At the beginning of each chapter, a set of pre-reading questions under the heading Think Before You Read helps to generate interest in the story, stimulate discussion, and activate students' prior knowledge. In addition, an illustration depicting a central moment in the story provides a visual representation of the content of the story.

A brief preview of the story (Story Preview) provides further preparation for reading and introduces students to some key vocabulary in the story. Students read the preview with a partner and practice guessing the meaning of highlighted words in context. In Using the Vocabulary, which follows, students work with a partner to complete a cloze passage with the vocabulary they have just learned. The cloze passage typically provides additional background information about the setting, plot, or theme.

Making Predictions further involves students in the story by asking them to predict part of the plot or what might happen to a character based on what they've discovered in the Story Preview. In a follow-up activity, Journal Writing, students write either about why they made their prediction or about feelings and experiences they've had that are closely related to a theme of the story.

A special Idioms and Expressions section helps students understand language whose meaning they would probably not figure out from its context in the story or find in the dictionary. A variety of strategies for using this section are possible. Some specific suggestions are provided in the Instructor's Manual.

At the end of the pre-reading section, students are introduced to a literary term, such as first person narrator or symbolism. The explanation of the term is followed by a Focus activity that guides students to look for examples of the target literary feature as they read. In this way, students both increase their understanding of literature and learn to read more attentively. Familiarity with literary terms also helps students discuss and write about the stories with greater ease.

READING THE STORY

Before reading a story, students should read the author's biography. Interesting information about each author's life is included, in addition to historical references to the period in which he or she lived.

It is best for students to read the stories first without looking up new words in the dictionary. During a second reading, students can note any words that trouble them and then discuss them with classmates, look them up, or get help from the instructor.

Post-Reading

The first of two sections following the story, After Reading, has students check and discuss their understanding of the story and work with the vocabulary and structures contained in the selection. The first activity in this section, Understanding the Story, provides comprehension questions. Next, work on vocabulary is provided in the Vocabulary Comprehension and Word Forms activities, which help students develop their vocabulary acquisition skills. A section on grammar explains a selected structure contained in the story, and a follow-up practice exercise helps students understand and master the target structure. Typically, phrases and sentences taken from the story are used to illustrate the structure, and in this way, the grammar focus helps students better understand the story.

The second post-reading section, Thinking About the Story, encourages students to analyze, discuss, and write about the story. Sharing Ideas gives students an opportunity to work with a partner or small group and relate the ideas in the story to their own knowledge and experience.

After Reading Between the Lines, an activity that focuses on inferential comprehension, students are asked to do some basic literary analysis in Analyzing the Story. This activity makes students reflect on literary features of the stories, introduced earlier in the Literary Term and Focus sections. Charts and other graphic organizers guide students through actual analyses of the stories and help them build on observations they have made while reading. The simplicity and straightforwardness of these graphic organizers ensure that the tasks are appropriate for students at this level. In a follow-up Pair Discussion, students correct and discuss their work.

The last activity in each chapter is Writing, which offers a choice of assignments, including one summary-writing activity for each story. Mostly focusing on the themes and plots of the stories, the writing activities provide a good balance of thought-provoking topics.

SUMMING UP

Each of the five parts of the text ends with a Summing Up section, which provides a basic review. The first activity, Take a Closer Look, invites students to make theme comparisons among the stories. Immediately following is a freewriting activity based on one of the themes. In Idioms and Expressions Review and Form Review, students practice using some of the idioms, expressions, and grammar they have learned.

APPENDIX

The Appendix consists of additional information on features of literature (in Elements of a Short Story), a set of review exercises for the entire text, a list of literary terms, a list of irregular verbs, and a section on spelling.

The Elements of a Short Story section is a useful resource that can be used with all of the stories in the text. After a brief explanation of the main story elements of setting, plot, characters, conflict, and theme, this section identifies all of these elements in chart format for the first story, "Eleven." For the following stories, a single blank worksheet is provided for students to copy into their notebooks or for instructors to photocopy and distribute. Doing this analysis will enable students to appreciate and understand each story more fully and improve their writing. Because it is more difficult than Analyzing the Story, instructors may wish to guide students through the first few chapters.

Discovering Fiction

STUDENT'S BOOK 1

Childhood Memories

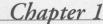

OUR CHILDHOOD memories affect us throughout our lives. Sometimes we have happy memories that make us smile in later years: warm times with parents and relatives or happy experiences with friends. Other memories, however, may be negative: illness, death, abuse, or separation from loved ones.

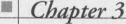 The stories in Part One explore traumatic events in the lives of three young children. As you read, consider how each child copes with the situation. You may recall similar experiences from your own childhood.

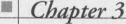 *Chapter 3*

THE BRACELET
— Yoshiko Uchida

Chapter 1

Eleven SANDRA CISNEROS

A | PRE-READING

1. Think Before You Read

Answer the following questions:

1. Have you ever been disappointed by your birthday? How did you feel about your birthday when you were a child? Did your birthday make you feel older?
2. Do you remember being embarrassed by a teacher when you were a child? What happened?
3. What are some things a child might do in a situation where an adult, who has more power, is being unfair to him or her?

2. Picture Focus

With a partner, talk about the picture. What do you think is happening?

3. Story Preview

Read the preview of the story and, with a partner, try to guess the meaning of the words in **bold** print.

Today is Rachel's eleventh birthday. As Rachel knows, when you're eleven, you're not just eleven. For example, sometimes you can feel like a dumb ten-year-old or like a **scared** five-year-old. Mrs. Price, Rachel's teacher, has found an ugly, old red sweater. Mrs. Price says that the sweater belongs to Rachel. When Rachel tries to tell Mrs. Price that the sweater isn't hers, Mrs. Price says this is **nonsense** and puts the sweater on Rachel's desk. Rachel can't do anything, and she feels very unhappy, even though it's her birthday. Rachel can't even **pretend** that she's not unhappy. She wishes that she could be **invisible** or far away.

4. Using the Vocabulary

Fill in the blanks below with the **bold** words from the Story Preview above. Then, with a partner, compare your answers.

Children love to make up stories and _____pretend_____ they are other people or animals. Some children even have a(n) _____ friend. The fact that no one else can see this friend doesn't make the friend seem less real to the child.

Sometimes, bad dreams can make children feel _____. When children tell adults they are afraid, the adults should take what the children say seriously; they should never treat it as _____.

5. Making Predictions

From the Story Preview, try to predict what will happen. Which of the following predictions do you think is the most *probable?* Circle your choice or give an answer that you think is better.

1. Rachel will be able to explain everything to Mrs. Price.

2. Mrs. Price will listen to Rachel.

3. Rachel will become more unhappy and cry.

4. Rachel will keep the sweater.

5. Rachel will have a good birthday.

6. _____

Journal Writing Write your predictions in your journal. Explain the reasons for your predictions.

IDIOMS AND EXPRESSIONS	
kind of partly, in a way **right away** immediately **that's enough** stop it	**getting mad** becoming angry **hold in** control or not show *(feelings)* **it's too late** because of what has or hasn't happened, the situation can't be OK now

6. Literary Term: First Person Narrator

"Eleven" has a **first person narrator.** This means that the story is told in the first person by the main character, Rachel, rather than in the third person, as many stories are. The first person narrator refers to him- or herself as "I." Because Rachel tells the story, we see what happens through her eyes. We get a clear sense, not just of what Rachel says and does, but also of how Rachel thinks, how she feels, and what she wishes for. We get to know Rachel.

Focus As you read "Eleven," ask yourself what you know about Rachel.

About the Author

Sandra Cisneros (1954–), the only daughter in a family of seven children, was born in Chicago. Her Mexican-American heritage, of which she is proud, is evident in many of her short stories. Cisneros has had a successful and varied career. In addition to being a poet and fiction writer, she has worked as an arts administrator and has taught students who had dropped out of high school. She has written four books of poetry and two books of short stories, *The House on Mango Street* and *Woman Hollering Creek*. In many of her short stories, such as "Eleven," Cisneros creates a view of the world through the eyes of a child. The language of these stories is simple and direct, but their ideas are serious and important.

Eleven

What they don't understand about birthdays and what they never tell you is that when you're eleven,
5 you're also ten, and nine, and eight, and seven, and six, and five, and four, and three, and two, and one. And when you wake up on your eleventh
10 birthday you expect to feel eleven, but you don't. You open your eyes and everything's just like yesterday, only it's today. And you don't feel eleven at all. You feel like you're still ten. And you
15 are – underneath the year that makes you eleven.

Like some days you might say something stupid, and that's the part of you that's still ten. Or maybe some days you might need to sit on your 20 mama's lap because you're scared, and that's the part of you that's five. And maybe one day when you're all grown up maybe you will need to cry like if you're three, and that's okay. That's 25 what I tell Mama when she's sad and needs to cry. Maybe she's feeling three.

Because the way you grow old is kind of like an onion or like the rings 30 inside a tree trunk or like my little wooden dolls that fit one inside the other, each year inside the next one. That's how being eleven years old is.

You don't feel eleven. Not right away. It takes a few days, weeks even, sometimes even months before you say Eleven when they ask you. And you don't feel smart eleven, not until you're almost twelve. That's the way it is.

Only today I wish I didn't have only eleven years rattling inside me like pennies in a tin Band-Aid box. Today I wish I was one hundred and two instead of eleven because if I was one hundred and two I'd have known what to say when Mrs. Price put the red sweater on my desk. I would've known how to tell her it wasn't mine instead of just sitting there with that look on my face and nothing coming out of my mouth.

"Whose is this?" Mrs. Price says, and she holds the red sweater up in the air for all the class to see. "Whose? It's been sitting in the coatroom for a month."

"Not mine," says everybody. "Not me."

"It has to belong to somebody," Mrs. Price keeps saying, but nobody can remember. It's an ugly sweater with red plastic buttons and a collar and sleeves all stretched out like you could use it for a jump rope. It's maybe a thousand years old and even if it belonged to me I wouldn't say so.

Maybe because I'm skinny, maybe because she doesn't like me, that stupid Sylvia Saldívar says, "I think it belongs to Rachel." An ugly sweater like that, all raggedy and old, but Mrs. Price believes her. Mrs. Price takes the sweater and puts it right on my desk, but when I open my mouth nothing comes out.

"That's not, I don't, you're not . . . Not mine," I finally say in a little voice that was maybe me when I was four.

"Of course it's yours," Mrs. Price says. "I remember you wearing it once." Because she's older and the teacher, she's right and I'm not.

Not mine, not mine, not mine, but Mrs. Price is already turning to page thirty-two, and math problem number four. I don't know why but all of a sudden I'm feeling sick inside, like the part of me that's three wants to come out of my eyes, only I squeeze them shut tight and bite down on my teeth real hard and try to remember today I am eleven, eleven. Mama is making a cake for me for tonight, and when Papa comes home everybody will sing Happy birthday, happy birthday to you.

But when the sick feeling goes away and I open my eyes, the red sweater's still sitting there like a big red mountain. I move the red sweater to the corner of my desk with my ruler. I move my pencil and books and eraser as far from it as possible. I even move my chair a little to the right. Not mine, not mine, not mine.

In my head I'm thinking how long till lunchtime, how long till I can take the red sweater and throw it over the schoolyard fence, or leave it hanging

"Of course it's yours," Mrs. Price says.

on a parking meter, or bunch it up into a little ball and toss it in the alley. Except when math period ends Mrs. Price says loud and in front of everybody, "Now, Rachel, that's enough," because she sees I've shoved the red sweater to the tippy-tip corner of my desk and it's hanging all over the edge like a waterfall, but I don't care.

"Rachel," Mrs. Price says. She says it like she's getting mad. "You put that sweater on right now and no more nonsense."

"But it's not –"

"Now!" Mrs. Price says.

This is when I wish I wasn't eleven, because all the years inside of me – ten, nine, eight, seven, six, five, four, three, two, and one – are pushing at the back of my eyes when I put one arm through one sleeve of the sweater that smells like cottage cheese, and then the other arm through the other and stand there with my arms apart like if the sweater hurts me and it does, all itchy and full of germs that aren't even mine.

That's when everything I've been holding in since this morning, since when Mrs. Price put the sweater on my desk, finally lets go, and all of a sudden I'm crying in front of everybody. I wish I was invisible but I'm not. I'm eleven and it's my birthday today and I'm crying like I'm three in front of everybody. I put my head down on the desk and bury my face in my stupid clown-sweater arms. My face all hot and spit coming out of my mouth because I can't stop the little animal noises from coming out of me, until there aren't any more tears left in my eyes, and it's just my body shaking like when you have the hiccups, and my whole head hurts like when you drink milk too fast.

But the worst part is right before the bell rings for lunch. That stupid Phyllis Lopez, who is even dumber than Sylvia Saldívar, says she remembers the red sweater is hers! I take it off right away and give it to her, only Mrs. Price pretends like everything's OK.

Today I'm eleven. There's a cake Mama's making for tonight, and when Papa comes home from work we'll eat it. There'll be candles and presents and everybody will sing Happy birthday, happy birthday to you, Rachel, only it's too late.

I'm eleven today. I'm eleven, ten, nine, eight, seven, six, five, four, three, two, and one, but I wish I was one hundred and two. I wish I was anything but eleven, because I want today to be far away already, far away like a runaway balloon, like a tiny *o* in the sky, so tiny-tiny you have to close your eyes to see it.

1. Understanding the Story

With a partner, answer these questions.

1. Where does the story take place?
2. Who is the narrator (the person telling the story)? How old is she?
3. Why is the day special to the narrator?
4. Why does Mrs. Price give Rachel the sweater?
5. What does the sweater look like?
6. What does Rachel plan to do with the sweater during lunchtime?
7. Why doesn't she do what she planned? What happens instead?
8. How does Rachel finally get rid of the sweater?
9. How does she feel at the end of the story?
10. According to Rachel, how is growing older similar to an onion or a tree with rings?

2. Vocabulary Comprehension

Choose the word from the following list that best completes each sentence below. Do not use the same word more than once.

alley	skinny	spit	raggedy
itchy	invisible	toss	pretend
scared	lap	hiccups	squeeze

1. A(n) _____lap_____ is a strange part of the body because you have it only

   when you are sitting down.

2. To get juice from a lemon, you have to _____ the lemon.

3. Children often get _____ when they hear stories about ghosts

   and monsters.

4. The red sweater wasn't comfortable because it felt _____.

5. The red sweater looked old and _____.

6. People who don't eat much are often _____.

7. With a microscope we can see many tiny things that to our eyes seem

   _____.

8. Rachel wanted to _____ the sweater over the fence.

9. In cities, some buildings have a(n) _____ between them.

10. The water we have in our mouths is called _____.

11. One way to stop _____ is to drink water and hold your breath.

12. Rachel couldn't _____ that she felt OK.

3. Word Forms

Complete the chart by filling in the various forms of the following words taken from "Eleven." An X indicates that no form is possible. Use your dictionary if you need help. **Note:** There may be more than one possible word for the same part of speech.

VERB	NOUN	ADJECTIVE	ADVERB
wish	_wish_		
scare			X
X	sadness		
X	stupidity		
X	loudness		
smell			X
itch			X

Work with a partner. Fill in the blanks in the story below with the appropriate words from your completed chart. Change the form of the word if necessary.

Tina says, "I want to be a famous singer someday." Tina _____ she could be famous right away, and she works very hard. Tina is a good singer, and her friends hope her _____ will come true.

4. *Grammar: Contractions*

Contractions are shortened forms of one or more words, made by leaving out letters. An apostrophe replaces the letters left out. Here are some common kinds of contractions with examples from the story:

Noun or pronoun plus a simple present form of the verb *be*

Example:
You open your eyes and everything's just like yesterday.

A form of *be, do, have,* or a modal (such as *can, should*) plus *not*

Examples:
The sweater's full of germs that aren't even mine.
You don't feel eleven at all.
I can't stop the little animal noises from coming out of me.

Noun or pronoun plus *will*

Example:
When Papa comes home from work we'll eat it.

Noun or pronoun plus present form of auxiliary verb *be (am, is, are)* or present or past form of auxiliary verb *have (have, has, had)*

Examples:
I'm feeling sick inside.
She sees I've shoved the red sweater to the tippy-tip corner of my desk.
That's when everything I've been holding in since this morning . . .
    finally lets go.

Past modals that include *have* (such as *should have, could have, would have*)

Example:
I would've known how to tell her it wasn't mine.

5. Application

Complete the following sentences from the story with the contraction for the words in parentheses. Then, with a partner, reread the story to find nine other sentences with contractions. List the sentences on a separate piece of paper, providing blanks and the full words in parentheses, as in the sentences here. Then give your sentences to another pair to complete. (To avoid using the same sentences, you can work with one half of the story and the other pair can work with the other half.)

1. _____That's_____ (That is) what I tell Mama when _____she's_____ (she is) sad and needs to cry.

2. I _____ (would have) known how to tell her it _____ (was not) mine.

3. _____ (It is) maybe a thousand years old and even if it belonged to me I _____ (would not) say so.

4. Maybe because _____ (I am) skinny, maybe because she _____ (does not) like me, that stupid Sylvia Saldívar says, "I think it belongs to Rachel."

5. "_____ (That is) not, I _____ (do not), _____ (you are) not . . . Not mine," I finally say.

6. The red _____ (sweater is) still sitting there like a big red mountain.

7. This is when I wish I _____ (was not) eleven.

8. _____ (There is) a cake _____ (Mama is) making for tonight.

9. _____ (There will) be candles and presents and everybody will sing Happy birthday, happy birthday to you, Rachel, only _____ (it is) too late.

1. Sharing Ideas

Discuss the following questions with a partner or in a group:

1. Do you agree with Rachel's idea that, no matter how old we are, we always have all the ages we have been inside of us? Why or why not?
2. If you were Mrs. Price, how would you have handled the situation with Rachel?
3. Why do you think Phyllis Lopez at first didn't say the sweater was hers?
4. How does Cisneros make us understand how Rachel feels? Give examples from the story of descriptions and language that helped you understand Rachel's feelings. Is the story believable – that is, do Rachel and her situation feel real to you?

2. Reading Between the Lines

Reading between the lines is an expression for understanding ideas that are not specifically stated. When you read between the lines, you infer things, that is, you figure things out from what the author does tell you.

Circle the letter of the answer that best completes each of the following sentences:

1. Rachel wishes she were 102 because
   a. at that age school and teachers like Mrs. Price would be in the distant past.
   b. at that age she wouldn't have an 11-year-old inside her.
   c. at that age she would have many older ages inside her.

2. In the end, when Phyllis has the sweater, Mrs. Price pretends everything is OK because
   a. she doesn't want Rachel to be upset.
   b. she doesn't want to admit she made a mistake.
   c. she doesn't want her class to be late for lunch.

3. Analyzing the Story

Look back at the Literary Term on page 6. What have you learned about Rachel as a result of her telling her own story? How much of this would you know if the story had a third person narrator, who could only tell you what Rachel said and did? Look at the story again and then make a chart like the one below and add examples to each category.

INFORMATION YOU LEARN FROM RACHEL AS NARRATOR	INFORMATION ANY NARRATOR COULD GIVE YOU
Rachel's ideas: *you have other ages inside you*	Rachel's words: *"That's not, I don't, you're not . . . Not mine."*
Rachel's feelings:	
Rachel's wants and wishes:	Rachel's actions:
Rachel's way of looking at the red sweater:	

Pair Discussion   With a partner, compare answers. Do you think you learned much more about Rachel because the story is told in the first person? Why or why not?

4. Writing

Choose one of the following writing assignments:

1. Write a summary of the story in two to three paragraphs. Be sure to include all the important events.
2. If you were Rachel, what would you have done? To answer this, write a dialogue between Rachel and Mrs. Price. Begin your dialogue with:
   Mrs. Price: Of course the sweater's yours. I remember you wearing it once. Continue the dialogue any way you want.
3. What sense do you have of Rachel from reading this story? Write a description of Rachel – how she looks, what she's like as a person, what her family is like, what she wants to do in the future – based on the information in the story and your imagination.

Chapter 2

The Blanket FLOYD DELL

PRE-READING

1. *Think Before You Read*

Answer the following questions:

1. What is a nursing home? Have you ever visited anyone in a nursing home?
2. Do you or did you have a grandparent you particularly loved or admired?
3. What are some of the things you enjoyed doing with that grandparent?
4. How are older people treated in your country?

2. *Picture Focus*

With a partner, talk about the picture. What do you think is happening?

3. Story Preview

Read the preview of the story and, with a partner, try to guess the meaning of the words in **bold** print.

Petey, an eleven-year-old boy, is unhappy because his father is sending Petey's grandfather to a **nursing home.** Petey is sad because this is the last evening he and Granddad will have together.

Petey is unhappy also because his father is going to marry a young woman who doesn't want an old man around the house. She thinks Granddad will be a **nuisance.** Petey's father doesn't really want to send Granddad away, but he wants to please his **fiancée.** He doesn't want to lose her.

The father buys Granddad a **blanket** to take with him to the nursing home so that he won't be cold at night. When the young woman sees the blanket, she becomes angry, and she **reproaches** Petey's father for buying it because she thinks it is too expensive.

4. Using the Vocabulary

Fill in the blanks below with the **bold** words from the Story Preview above. Then, with a partner, compare your answers. Change the form of the word if necessary.

When they rarely receive visits from their children or others, many older people in

___nursing homes___ become bored and unhappy. Sometimes, a parent is sent

away because the family feels that the parent is a _____ and that

caring for him or her is too much trouble. Children living with older parents can

become impatient with them as the parents begin to forget things. Unpleasant

scenes can result when children _____ their parents for small

mistakes, such as tearing a _____ or another part of the parent's

bed. Sometimes, a man who lives with an older parent becomes more impatient

when he plans to get married. A difficult moment for the man might come when

he has to introduce his parent to his _____.

5. Making Predictions

From the Story Preview, try to predict what Petey's father will do. Which of the following predictions do you think is the most *probable?* Circle your choice or give an answer that you think is better.

1. Petey's father will take the blanket back to the store.

2. He will keep his father at home.

3. He will break his engagement.

4. He will persuade his fiancée to change her mind.

5. He will feel ashamed of himself.

6. _____

Journal Writing   In your journal, explain why you chose your answer.

IDIOMS AND EXPRESSIONS	
fetch get, bring	**take (myself) off** go away
tune up adjust the strings of a musical instrument so it has the right sound	**eyes cast down** looking down
	a huff a fit of anger
	come in handy be useful later
slobbered acted excessively affectionate	

6. Literary Term: Poetic Justice

In real life, people don't necessarily get what they deserve. Sometimes, good people have bad things happen to them, and bad people have good things happen. However, in fiction, authors can reward or punish characters for their actions. This is called **poetic justice** (because it is literary and the characters get what they deserve).

Focus   When you read "The Blanket," ask yourself if each character gets what he or she deserves.

About the Author

Born in Illinois, Floyd Dell (1887–1969) moved to New York City when he was in his twenties. There he joined a number of radical causes and lived in Greenwich Village, where he associated with writers, actors, and painters. Dell wrote novels, plays, and short stories, in addition to his autobiography, *Homecoming*. In most of his fiction, Dell shows sympathy for the poor and underprivileged, especially the aged, as you will see when you read "The Blanket."

The Blanket

 Petey hadn't really believed that Dad would be doing it – sending Granddad away. "Away"
5 was what they were calling it. Not until now could he believe it of Dad.

But here was the blanket that Dad had that day bought for him, and in
10 the morning he'd be going away. And this was the last evening they'd be having together. Dad was off seeing that girl he was to marry. He'd not be back till late, and they could sit up and
15 talk.

It was a fine September night, with a thin white moon riding high over the gully. When they'd washed up the supper dishes they went out on the
20 shanty porch, the old man and the bit of a boy, taking their chairs. "I'll get me fiddle," said the old man, "and play ye some of the old tunes." But instead of the fiddle he brought out the blanket. It was a big, double blanket, red, with 25 black cross stripes.

"Now, isn't that a fine blanket!" said the old man, smoothing it over his knees. "And isn't your father a kind man to be giving the old fellow a 30 blanket like that to go away with? It cost something, it did – look at the wool of it! And warm it will be these cold winter nights to come. There'll be few blankets there the equal of this 35 one!"

It was like Granddad to be saying that. He was trying to make it easier. He'd pretended all along it was he that was wanting to go away to the great 40 brick building – the government place, where he'd be with so many other old fellows having the best of everything. . . . But Petey hadn't believed Dad would really do it, until this night when he brought home the blanket.

"Oh, yes, it's a fine blanket," said Petey, and got up and went into the shanty. He wasn't the kind to cry, and besides, he was too old for that, being eleven. He'd just come in to fetch Granddad's fiddle.

The blanket slid to the floor as the old man took the fiddle and stood up. It was the last night they'd be having together. There wasn't any need to say, "Play all the old tunes." Granddad tuned up for a minute, and then said, "This is one you'll like to remember."

The thin moon was high overhead, and there was a gentle breeze playing down the gully. He'd never be hearing Granddad play like this again. It was as well Dad was moving into that new house, away from here. He'd not want, Petey wouldn't, to sit here on the old porch of fine evenings, with Granddad gone.

The tune changed. "Here's something gayer." Petey sat and stared out over the gully. Dad would marry that girl. Yes, that girl who'd kissed him and slobbered over him, saying she'd try to be a good mother to him, and all. . . . His chair creaked as he involuntarily gave his body a painful twist.

The tune stopped suddenly, and

■   ■   ■

It was the last night they'd be having together.

■   ■   ■

Granddad said: "It's a poor tune, except to be dancing to." And then: "It's a fine girl your father's going to marry. He'll be feeling young again, with a pretty wife like that. And what would an old fellow like me be doing around their house, getting in the way, an old nuisance, what with my talk of aches and pains! And then there'll be babies coming, and I'd not want to be there to hear them crying at all hours. It's best that I take myself off, like I'm doing. One more tune or two, and then we'll be going to bed to get some sleep against the morning, when I'll pack up my fine blanket and take my leave. Listen to this, will you? It's a bit sad, but a fine tune for a night like this."

They didn't hear the two people coming down the gully path, Dad and the pretty girl with the hard, bright face like a china doll's. But they heard her laugh, right by the porch, and the tune stopped on a wrong, high, startled note. Dad didn't say anything, but the girl came forward and spoke to Granddad prettily: "I'll not be seeing you leave in the morning, so I came over to say good-bye."

"It's kind of you," said Granddad, with his eyes cast down; and then, seeing the blanket at his feet, he stooped to pick it up. "And will you look at this," he said in embarrassment, "the fine blanket my son has given me to go away with!"

"Yes," she said, "it's a fine blanket."

She felt of the wool, and repeated in surprise, "A fine blanket – I'll say it is!" She turned to Dad, and said to him coldly, "It cost something, that."

He cleared his throat, and said defensively, "I wanted him to have the best. . . ."

The girl stood there, still intent on the blanket. "It's double, too," she said reproachfully to Dad.

"Yes," said Granddad, "it's double – a fine blanket for an old fellow to be going away with."

The boy went abruptly into the shanty. He was looking for something. He could hear that girl reproaching Dad, and Dad becoming angry in his slow way. And now she was suddenly going away in a huff. . . . As Petey came out, she turned and called back, "All the same, he doesn't need a double blanket!" And she ran up the gully path.

Dad was looking after her uncertainly.

"Oh, she's right," said the boy coldly. "Here, Dad" – and he held out a pair of scissors. "Cut the blanket in two."

Both of them stared at the boy, startled. "Cut it in two, I tell you, Dad!" he cried out. "And keep the other half!"

"That's not a bad idea," said Granddad gently. "I don't need so much of a blanket."

"Yes," said the boy harshly, "a single blanket's enough for an old man when he's sent away. We'll save the other half, Dad; it will come in handy later."

"Now, what do you mean by that?" asked Dad.

"I mean," said the boy slowly, "that I'll give it to you, Dad – when you're old and I'm sending you – away."

There was a silence, and then Dad went over to Granddad and stood before him, not speaking. But Granddad understood, for he put out a hand and laid it on Dad's shoulder. Petey was watching them. And he heard Granddad whisper, "It's all right, son – I knew you didn't mean it. . . ." And then Petey cried.

But it didn't matter – because they were all three crying together.

1. Understanding the Story

With a partner, answer these questions.

1. Why is Granddad being sent away?
2. How old is Petey?
3. What makes Petey realize that Granddad is really going to the nursing home?
4. What excuses does Granddad make for his son's plan to send him away?
5. How would you describe the woman that Petey's father intends to marry?
6. Do you think Dad will change his mind about sending Granddad away? Find sentences from the story that support your opinion.

2. Vocabulary Comprehension

Read each of the following sentences. Then circle the letter of the answer that gives the correct meaning for each word in **bold** print.

1. Granddad's blanket **slid** to the floor.
   - a. was pushed
   - b. fell
   - c. was thrown
   - d. lay

2. Petey went to fetch Granddad's **fiddle.**
   - a. harmonica
   - b. bugle
   - c. violin
   - d. ukulele

3. His chair **creaked.**
   - a. sagged
   - b. broke
   - c. stiffened
   - d. squeaked

4. He **involuntarily** gave his body a painful twist.
   - a. deliberately
   - b. unintentionally
   - c. rudely
   - d. consciously

5. Granddad and Petey were **startled** by the girl's laugh.
   - a. frightened
   - b. pleased
   - c. disgusted
   - d. surprised

6. She spoke **reproachfully** to Petey's father about the cost of the blanket.
   a. pleadingly
   b. in a scolding manner
   c. unpleasantly
   d. indifferently

7. Petey went into the **shanty** to get the fiddle.
   a. garage
   b. attic
   c. shack
   d. porch

8. Petey's voice was **harsh** when he told his father to cut the blanket in half.
   a. rough
   b. soft
   c. gentle
   d. cold

9. Granddad felt that he had become a **nuisance** in the house.
   a. too old
   b. an annoyance
   c. not understanding
   d. a financial burden

10. Petey's father spoke **defensively** about buying an expensive blanket for his father.
    a. with conviction
    b. uncaringly
    c. excusing himself
    d. accusing others

11. Granddad **stooped** to pick up the blanket.
    a. sat down
    b. moved away
    c. bent over
    d. got up

12. Granddad was **embarrassed** to talk about the blanket in front of Dad's fiancée.
    a. uncomfortable
    b. unable
    c. unhappy
    d. uncertain

13. Petey **abruptly** went inside to look for the scissors.
    a. quickly
    b. suddenly
    c. slowly
    d. gently

14. Granddad didn't want people to hear him complain about his **aches** and pains.
    a. continuous pain
    b. sudden pain
    c. bad pain
    d. mild pain

3. Word Forms

Complete the chart by filling in the various forms of the following words taken from "The Blanket." Use your dictionary if you need help. **Note:** There may be more than one possible word for the same part of speech.

VERB	NOUN	ADJECTIVE	ADVERB
reproach	*reproach*	_____	_____
pretend	_____	_____	_____
pain	_____	_____	_____
sleep	_____	_____	_____
startle	_____	_____	_____
_____	intent	_____	_____

Work with a partner. Find at least three other verbs in "The Blanket" and write their various word forms in a chart like the one above. Then write sentences using these words as adjectives, adverbs, or nouns.

4. Grammar: Phrasal Verbs

A phrasal verb (also called a two-word verb) is a combination of a verb and a preposition or adverb.

Examples:
Petey's father intends to send Granddad **away**.
Granddad **tuned up** his fiddle.
Petey **got up** and went **into** the shanty.

Some phrasal verbs can be separated by a noun or pronoun.

Example:
Petey hadn't really believed that Dad would be . . . **sending** Granddad
    away.

Other phrasal verbs cannot be separated.

Examples:
Dad's fiancée ran up the path.
The students came across a good story.

5. Application

Reread the story to look for other examples of phrasal verbs. Then work with a partner to guess the meaning of the phrasal verbs and complete the following chart. The first two examples have been done for you.

PHRASAL VERB	MEANING	SENTENCE
washed up went out	washed the dishes after eating left the house	When they'd washed up the supper dishes, they went out on the shanty porch.

Now write three sentences with the phrasal verbs you found.

1. _____

_____

2. _____

_____

3. _____

_____

1. *Sharing Ideas*

Discuss the following questions with a partner or in a group:

1. Why does Petey dislike the woman that his father intends to marry?
2. Do you think that Petey's father will ever marry his fiancée? Why or why not?
3. What is the real reason that Petey's father bought the blanket?
4. Nice people sometimes do unkind things. Give an example from your own experience or from another story you have read.
5. What lesson do you think Petey's father learned? In your opinion, did the fiancée get what she deserved?

2. *Reading Between the Lines*

Being a good reader involves *reading between the lines.* This means coming to a conclusion from the facts given in a story or text. For example, in "The Blanket," the author does not tell us that Petey's father has changed his mind about sending Granddad to the nursing home, but we conclude this since the story ends with the sentence, "They were all three crying together."

Practice reading between the lines. Circle the letter of the answer that best completes each of the following statements:

1. We can assume that Petey's father intended to send Granddad away because
   a. he had no regard for his father's happiness.
   b. he believed that Granddad would be happier in a nursing home.
   c. he was easily influenced by his fiancée.

2. We can assume that the fiancée objected to the gift of the blanket because
   a. she wanted the money for herself.
   b. she didn't like Granddad.
   c. she wanted to keep the money for Petey.

3. When the author describes Dad's fiancée as "the pretty girl with the hard, bright face like a china doll's," he wants to emphasize
   a. her beauty.
   b. her delicacy.
   c. her lack of kindness.

3. Analyzing the Story

Look back at the Literary Term on page 18. Think of some examples of poetic justice in this story. Make a chart like the one below and list each character's actions in the second column. Then list the things that happen to each character in the third column.

CHARACTER	WHAT THE CHARACTER DOES	WHAT HAPPENS TO HIM OR HER AT THE END
Petey	shows his anger about Dad sending Granddad away	Granddad stays home with him and Dad.
Granddad		
Dad		
The fiancée		

Pair Discussion   With a partner, compare what you have written in your charts. Correct any mistakes you find. Then think about what happens to each character at the end. Is it an example of poetic justice? Why or why not?

4. Writing

Choose one of the following writing assignments:

1. Write a summary of the story in two or three paragraphs. Make sure to include all of the major events. Look at the chart above if you need help.
2. Why do some people cry when they're happy? Write a short composition about an experience when you or someone you knew cried for joy.
3. Make up a conversation between Petey and Granddad the morning after the incident with the blanket.
4. People often buy gifts to cover up a guilty feeling. Compare the father's gift to Granddad with a present that was given to you because someone else felt guilty.
5. Discuss some of the problems grown children sometimes face with their parents. What problems do parents have relating to adult children?

Chapter 3

The Bracelet YOSHIKO UCHIDA

A PRE-READING

1. Think Before You Read

Answer the following questions:

1. How would you feel if you had to leave your home permanently?
2. What would you miss the most if you had to leave home?
3. What is a concentration camp? Give some examples you have heard of.
4. What have you heard about concentration camps in the United States?

2. Picture Focus

With a partner, talk about the picture. What do you think is happening?

3. Story Preview

Read the preview of the story and, with a partner, try to guess the meaning of the words in **bold** print.

Ruri, a Japanese-American girl, and her family were **evacuated** from their home during World War II. At that time, the United States was at war with Japan. The U.S. government forced many Japanese Americans and their Japanese-born parents to leave their homes and live in special **camps.**

The Japanese-American children were born in the United States, so they were U.S. citizens. Their parents, however, were **aliens,** not citizens. The government **interned** Japanese-American families in camps because U.S. politicians thought that they might be working for Japan as spies.

On the day Ruri had to leave home for the camp, her best friend gave her a **bracelet.** Ruri wore the bracelet on the day she left, and it reminded her of her best friend.

4. Using the Vocabulary

Fill in the blanks below with the **bold** words from the Story Preview above. Then, with a partner, compare your answers.

Most people living in the United States today are U.S. citizens, but many others

are _____ aliens _____. During World War II, citizenship was a serious

question. However, even certain people born in America – people with U.S.

citizenship – were distrusted by the government, which thought that

many Americans of Japanese origin were spies. Japanese Americans were

_____ from their homes by the army. The government made them

live in _____, like prisoners of war. The Japanese Americans were

_____ in these places until the war was over, and then they were

released. Naturally, people who are forced to leave their homes value even small

objects that remind them of home and their loved ones. Jewelry – for example,

a(n) _____ that can be worn on the wrist – takes on great

importance at such times.

5. Making Predictions

Read the first five paragraphs of "The Bracelet" (lines 1–36) and think about what might happen to Ruri and her family. Which of the following predictions do you think is most *probable?* Circle your choice or give an answer that you think is better.

1. Ruri and her family will go to a new home of their own.

2. They will be separated.

3. They will return to their home very soon.

4. They will never return home.

5. _____

Journal Writing In your journal, explain why you made your predictions. Then read the rest of the story.

IDIOMS AND EXPRESSIONS	
junk things that aren't worth very much	**I'll say** I agree (in certain contexts)
evacuated removed	**a slip of paper** a piece of paper
interned put in prison	**fix it up** make something attractive
aliens foreigners	**set up** get something in order
duffel bag canvas bag to hold items	**go over** repeat, review
	never mind don't be upset, don't bother

6. Literary Term: Setting

The **setting** of a story is the time and location in which it takes place. Often, the setting of a story has a causal relationship with the events of the story. The setting of this story – the United States during World War II – is the basis for the entire plot.

Focus As you read the story, look for all the details that describe the setting.

About the Author

Yoshiko Uchida (1921–1992) was born in California and grew up in Berkeley. After Pearl Harbor was bombed, her father was imprisoned, and the rest of her family was sent to a camp in Utah. This experience provides the background for "The Bracelet." Uchida once commented, "I want to give young Asians a sense of their past . . . and to non-Asians, the picture of Japanese as real people." Among the author's novels are *Journey to Topaz* and *Picture Bride*.

The Bracelet

"Mama, is it time to go?"

I hadn't planned to cry, but the tears came suddenly, and I wiped them away with the back of my hand. I didn't want my older sister to see me crying.

"It's almost time, Ruri," my mother said gently. Her face was filled with a kind of sadness I had never seen before.

I looked around at my empty room. The clothes that Mama always told me to hang up in the closet, the junk piled on my dresser, the old rag doll I could never bear to part with; they were all gone. There was nothing left in my room, and there was nothing left in the rest of the house. The rugs and furniture were gone, the pictures and drapes were down, and the closets and cupboards were empty. The house was like a gift box after the nice thing inside was gone; just a lot of nothingness.

It was almost time to leave our home, but we weren't moving to a nicer house or to a new town. It was April 21, 1942. The United States and Japan were at war, and every Japanese person on the West Coast was being evacuated by the government to a concentration camp. Mama, my sister Keiko, and I were being sent from our home, and out of Berkeley, and eventually, out of California.

The doorbell rang, and I ran to answer it before my sister could. I thought maybe by some miracle, a messenger from the government might be standing there, tall and proper and buttoned into a uniform, come to tell us it was all a terrible mistake; that we wouldn't have to leave after all. Or maybe the messenger would have a telegram from Papa, who was interned in a prisoner-of-war camp in Montana because he had worked for a Japanese business firm.

The FBI had come to pick up Papa and hundreds of other Japanese community leaders on the very day that Japanese planes had bombed Pearl Harbor. The government thought they were dangerous enemy aliens. If it weren't so sad, it would have been funny. Papa could no more be dangerous than the mayor of our city, and he was every bit as loyal to the United States. He had lived here since 1917.

When I opened the door, it wasn't a messenger from anywhere. It was my best friend, Laurie Madison, from next door. She was holding a package wrapped up like a birthday present, but she wasn't wearing her party dress, and her face drooped like a wilted tulip.

"Hi," she said. "I came to say good-bye."

She thrust the present at me and told me it was something to take to camp. "It's a bracelet," she said before I could open the package. "Put it on so you won't have to pack it." She knew I didn't have one inch of space left in my suitcase. We had been instructed to take only what we could carry into camp, and Mama had told us that we could each take only two suitcases.

"Then how are we ever going to pack the dishes and blankets and sheets they've told us to bring with us?" Keiko worried.

"I don't really know," Mama said, and she simply began packing those big impossible things into an enormous duffel bag — along with umbrellas, boots, a kettle, hot plate, and flashlight.

"Who's going to carry that huge sack?" I asked.

But Mama didn't worry about things like that. "Someone will help us," she said. "Don't worry." So I didn't.

Laurie wanted me to open her package and put on the bracelet before she left. It was a thin gold chain with a heart dangling on it. She helped me put it on, and I told her I'd never take it off, ever.

■ ■ ■

She helped me put it on, and I told her I'd never take it off, ever.

■ ■ ■

"Well, good-bye then," Laurie said awkwardly. "Come home soon."

"I will," I said, although I didn't know if I would ever get back to Berkeley again.

I watched Laurie go down the block, her long blond pigtails bouncing as she walked. I wondered who would be sitting in my desk at Lincoln Junior High now that I was gone. Laurie kept turning and waving, even walking backwards for a while, until she got to the corner. I didn't want to watch anymore, and I slammed the door shut.

The next time the doorbell rang, it

was Mrs. Simpson, our other neighbor. She was going to drive us to the Congregational church, which was the Civil Control Station where all the Japanese of Berkeley were supposed to report.

It was time to go. "Come on, Ruri. Get your things," my sister called to me.

It was a warm day, but I put on a sweater and my coat so I wouldn't have to carry them, and I picked up my two suitcases. Each one had a tag with my name and our family number on it. Every Japanese family had to register and get a number. We were Family Number 13453.

Mama was taking one last look around our house. She was going from room to room, as though she were trying to take a mental picture of the house she had lived in for fifteen years, so she would never forget it.

I saw her take a long last look at the garden that Papa loved. The irises beside the fish pond were just beginning to bloom. If Papa had been home, he would have cut the first iris blossom and brought it inside to Mama. "This one is for you," he would have said. And Mama would have smiled and said, "Thank you, Papa San,"[1] and put it in her favorite cut-glass vase.

But the garden looked shabby and forsaken now that Papa was gone and Mama was too busy to take care of it. It looked the way I felt, sort of empty and lonely and abandoned.

When Mrs. Simpson took us to the Civil Control Station, I felt even worse. I was scared, and for a minute I thought I was going to lose my breakfast right in front of everybody. There must have been over a thousand Japanese people gathered at the church. Some were old and some were young. Some were talking and laughing, and some were crying. I guess everybody else was scared too. No one knew exactly what was going to happen to us. We just knew we were being taken to the Tanforan Racetracks, which the army had turned into a camp for the Japanese. There were fourteen other camps like ours along the West Coast.

What scared me most were the soldiers standing at the doorway of the church hall. They were carrying guns with mounted bayonets. I wondered if they thought we would try to run away, and whether they'd shoot us or come after us with their bayonets if we did.

A long line of buses waited to take us to camp. There were trucks, too, for our baggage. And Mama was right; some men were there to help us load our duffel bag. When it was time to board the buses, I sat with Keiko and Mama sat behind us. The bus went down Grove Street and passed the small Japanese food store where Mama used to order her bean-curd cakes and pickled radish. The windows were all boarded up, but there was a sign still hanging on the door that read, "We are loyal Americans."

The crazy thing about the whole

---

[1] *Papa San:* In Japan, the suffix *san* is added to a name as a mark of respect.

evacuation was that we were all loyal Americans. Most of us were citizens because we had been born here. But our parents, who had come from Japan, couldn't become citizens because there was a law that prevented any Asian from becoming a citizen. Now everybody with a Japanese face was being shipped off to concentration camps.

"It's stupid," Keiko muttered as we saw the racetrack looming up beside the highway. "If there were any Japanese spies around, they'd have gone back to Japan long ago."

"I'll say," I agreed. My sister was in high school and she ought to know, I thought.

When the bus turned into Tanforan, there were more armed guards at the gate, and I saw barbed wire strung around the entire grounds. I felt as though I were going into a prison, but I hadn't done anything wrong.

We streamed off the buses and poured into a huge room, where doctors looked down our throats and peeled back our eyelids to see if we had any diseases. Then we were given our housing assignments. The man in charge gave Mama a slip of paper. We were in Barrack 16, Apartment 40.

"Mama!" I said. "We're going to live in an apartment!" The only apartment I had ever seen was the one my piano teacher lived in. It was in an enormous building in San Francisco with an elevator and thick carpeted hallways. I thought how wonderful it would be to have our own elevator. A house was all right, but an apartment seemed elegant and special.

We walked down the racetrack looking for Barrack 16. Mr. Noma, a friend of Papa's, helped us carry our bags. I was so busy looking around, I slipped and almost fell on the muddy track. Army barracks had been built everywhere, all around the racetrack and even in the center oval.

Mr. Noma pointed beyond the track toward the horse stables. "I think your barrack is out there."

He was right. We came to a long stable that had once housed the horses of Tanforan, and we climbed up the wide ramp. Each stall had a number painted on it, and when we got to 40, Mr. Noma pushed open the door.

"Well, here it is," he said, "Apartment 40."

The stall was narrow and empty and dark. There were two small windows on each side of the door. Three folded army cots were on the dust-covered floor and one light bulb dangled from the ceiling. That was all. This was our apartment, and it still smelled of horses.

Mama looked at my sister and then at me. "It won't be so bad when we fix it up," she began. "I'll ask Mrs. Simpson to send me some material for curtains. I could make some cushions too, and . . . well . . ." She stopped. She

This was our apartment, and it still smelled of horses.

couldn't think of anything more to say.

Mr. Noma said he'd go get some mattresses for us. "I'd better hurry before they're all gone." He rushed off. I think he wanted to leave so that he wouldn't have to see Mama cry. But he needn't have run off, because Mama didn't cry. She just went out to borrow a broom and began sweeping out the dust and dirt. "Will you girls set up the cots?" she asked.

It was only after we'd put up the last cot that I noticed my bracelet was gone. "I've lost Laurie's bracelet!" I screamed. "My bracelet's gone!"

We looked all over the stall and even down the ramp. I wanted to run back down the track and go over every inch of ground we'd walked on, but it was getting dark and Mama wouldn't let me.

I thought of what I'd promised Laurie. I wasn't ever going to take the bracelet off, not even when I went to take a shower. And now I had lost it on my very first day in camp. I wanted to cry.

I kept looking for it all the time we were in Tanforan. I didn't stop looking until the day we were sent to another camp, called Topaz, in the middle of a desert in Utah. And then I gave up.

But Mama told me never mind. She said I didn't need a bracelet to remember Laurie, just as I didn't need anything to remember Papa or our home in Berkeley or all the people and things we loved and had left behind.

"Those are things we can carry in our hearts and take with us no matter where we are sent," she said.

And I guess she was right. I've never forgotten Laurie, even now.

1. *Understanding the Story*

With a partner, answer these questions.

1. Where do Ruri and her family live?
2. Why do they have to leave their home?
3. Where is Ruri's father?
4. How many possessions can the family take with them?
5. Where is Ruri's family assigned to live?
6. Why is Ruri upset when she loses the bracelet? What does the bracelet mean to her?
7. How does Ruri's mother comfort her when Ruri loses the bracelet?

2. *Vocabulary Comprehension*

Choose the word from the following list that best completes each sentence below. Do not use the same word more than once.

piled	irises	suspected	enormous
abandoned	elegant	oval	cots
drapes	droop	stall	

1. Flowers begin to _____ *droop* _____ if you don't give them enough water.

2. We just bought new _____ to hang on the large living room window.

3. Dressed in her beautiful white satin wedding gown, the bride looked

   _____ .

4. My dining room table is in the shape of a(n) _____ , almost like an egg.

5. At the racetrack, each horse is kept in a(n) _____ before the race.

6. When I was a child at summer camp, we didn't have any regular beds. We slept

   on _____ .

7. In wartime, people of foreign birth are often unfairly _____ of being spies for the enemy.

8. The mother told her son, "Please hang your clothes in the closet. They are _____ up on your bed."

9. Ann's husband was unfaithful for a long time, and he finally _____ his wife and children.

10. _____ are beautiful purple flowers that bloom in the spring.

11. Limousines are often so _____ that they can't be parked in a typical parking space on a city street.

3. Word Forms

Complete the chart by filling in the various forms of the following words taken from "The Bracelet." An X indicates that no form is possible. Use your dictionary if you need help. **Note:** There may be more than one possible word for the same part of speech.

VERB	NOUN	ADJECTIVE	ADVERB
dangle	_____	_dangling_	X
droop	_____	_____	_____
thrust	_____	_____	X
_____	drapes	_____	X
X	_____	elegant	_____
abandon	_____	_____	X
pile	_____	_____	X
suspect	_____	_____	X

Work with a partner. Using some of the adjectives and verbs from "The Bracelet," write a description of Ruri's "Apartment 40" after her mother fixed it up.

4. Grammar: The Past Tense: Simple Versus Continuous

The past continuous is used for an action taking place over a longer period of time than another action taking place during that time period.

Example:

        SIMPLE PAST   PAST CONTINUOUS

When Ruri saw Laurie, she was holding a package.

The past continuous is formed with the past of *be (was/were)* plus the *-ing* form of the verb.

Example:

Some were talking and laughing. . . .

We often use the past continuous and the simple past in the same sentence to show that something happened in the middle of something else.

Example:

They were moving when Sam called.

(Moving is a longer action, which was taking place when Sam called.)

Note: **Certain verbs are typically not used in the continuous form. Some of these verbs are the following:** *know, want, need, like, love, hate, seem, believe,* **and** *hear.*

5. Application

Complete the sentences below with the simple past or the past continuous.

Example:

When I **came** (come) home, my cat **was chewing** (chew) the living
    room rug.
(The cat was still chewing the rug.)

1. What _____*were*_____ you _____*doing*_____ (do) at 10 o'clock last night?

2. I _____ (study) English.

3. Last year at this time, Mario _____ (live) in Italy.

4. Jose _____ (come) to the United States in 1994.

5. It _____ (snow) eight times last winter.

6. It _____ (snow) when I _____ (get) up this morning.

7. I _____ (hear) the phone ring when I _____ (take) a shower.

8. Dorothy _____ (cut) herself while she _____ (peel) potatoes.

9. We _____ (talk) about him before he _____ (arrive).

10. When I _____ (see) her, she _____ (plant) flowers in the garden.

11. While I _____ (live) in California, I often _____ (go) to Hawaii for vacation.

12. It _____ (start) to rain when I _____ (run) this morning.

13. It _____ (still, rain) when I _____ (leave) for work.

Editing Practice Edit the following paragraphs by correcting any verb that is used in the wrong tense:

When I was meeting my friend Blanca, she studied to be an actress. She was wanting me to study acting, too, but I wasn't believing I would be good at it. I was knowing Blanca would be good, and I thought she would be getting a good part in some play and become successful.

Then I wasn't hearing anything from Blanca for a long time. Finally, she called to tell me she took classes and was going to become a teacher. When she was calling me, I was going to work and couldn't speak to her. But she said she did very well so far in her studies.

1. Sharing Ideas

Discuss the following questions with a partner or in a group:

1. With your classmates, discuss some of the unjust decisions that governments make during wartime.
2. Why is the sign "We are loyal Americans" a sad contrast to the way the Japanese Americans are treated in the story?
3. Why is Ruri excited when she thinks she is going to live in an apartment? How is she disappointed?
4. Describe the place to which the family has been assigned.
5. Give three examples of Mama's courage. Find sentences from the story to support your answer.
6. Why would it have been impossible for the author to have written this story if the action had occurred in another period of American history?

2. Reading Between the Lines

Practice reading between the lines. Circle the letter of the answer that best completes each of the following statements:

1. We can assume that Laurie was sad when she came to Ruri's house to say good-bye because
   a. she wasn't wearing her party dress.
   b. her face drooped like a wilted tulip.
   c. she brought Ruri a present.

2. From her behavior, we can conclude that Ruri's mother
   a. survived the camp.
   b. felt she would never see her husband again.
   c. could not cope with the situation.

3. We can assume that Mrs. Simpson
   a. was a good friend to Ruri's family.
   b. was in charge of the evacuation of the Japanese.
   c. was not helpful to the family.

3. Analyzing the Story

Look back at the Literary Term on page 30. Make a chart like the one below and find the details that describe the setting of the camp. Fill in those details in the left column. Then think about what those details tell you about the setting and list your conclusions in the column to the right.

SETTING DETAILS	WHAT THE DETAILS TELL YOU ABOUT THE SETTING
There are armed guards and barbed wire at the gate.	The camp is like a prison.

Pair Discussion   With a partner, compare what you have written in your charts. Correct any mistakes you find. Then think about the way the setting changes from the beginning to the end of the story. What kinds of changes can you find? What do the changes tell you?

4. Writing

Choose one of the following writing assignments:

1. Write a summary of the part of the story that takes place in the camp in two to three paragraphs. Make sure to include the most important points. Use some of the information from the chart above if you need help.
2. Pretend you are Laurie. Write a letter to your friend Ruri a week after the evacuation.
3. Do you think Ruri will ever see Laurie again? If so, describe their meeting with one another.
4. Ruri's mother has the ability to make the best of a bad situation. Do you have any family member or friend who is like her? Describe that person and give examples of his or her strength of character.

Summing Up

A | TAKE A CLOSER LOOK

1. Theme Comparison: Loneliness

Loneliness is a theme in all the stories in Part One. There is a difference between being alone and feeling lonely. We may feel lonely even though we are surrounded by people. Ruri describes herself as being like the garden, "sort of empty and lonely and abandoned." Compare Ruri's loneliness in "The Bracelet" with Rachel's in "Eleven."

1. How does each girl deal with her feelings?
2. Do other people help them cope with their feelings?
3. What does the bracelet mean to Ruri?
4. What does the sweater mean to Rachel?

2. Freewriting

Write the word *loneliness* on the top of a sheet of paper. Now write any words that come into your mind when you think of this word. For fifteen minutes, write about a time in your life when you felt lonely. What were the circumstances? How did you deal with the situation?

B | REVIEW

1. Idioms and Expressions Review

The following story will use some of the idioms you learned in Part One. Work with a partner or in a small group. Fill in the blanks with the correct idioms and expressions. The first letter of each answer is supplied.

duffel bag	never mind	I'll say	getting mad
go over	slip of paper	fix it up	huff
set up	come in handy	junk	

Bob and his sister, Rita, bought an old house in the country. They drove to the house and when they arrived, they found a lot of things left by the previous owners. The next day, they started cleaning up all the j_unk___ that had been left in the basement.

Bob said, "There's a lot of work to do in this house."

Rita agreed. "I'_____ _____. We'll have to work day and night to f_____ _____ _____ before we can s_____ _____ our furniture. It would be nice to have some help. In fact, a couple of brooms and a vacuum cleaner would c_____ _____ _____."

Bob said, "N_____ _____ the mess. It's not important. Let's g_____ _____ the list of things we have to do. Then I'll make some lunch."

Rita asked, "Where's that s_____ _____ _____ I wrote everything on?"

Bob answered, "I think it's in my d_____ _____. I'll get it when I have a chance."

Rita was impatient. She said, "Will you hurry, Bob? I'm g_____ _____."

He answered, "Relax, Rita. If we're going to get the job done, we shouldn't get in a h_____ with each other." Rita replied, "OK, Bob, you're right. Let's get to work."

2. *Form Review*

Read the following paragraph. On a separate piece of paper, write the appropriate contraction for each of the **bold** words or phrases.

> **I am** sorry that I **cannot** attend the concert. I **have not** been able to obtain tickets because the box office **is not** open before ten o'clock. I hope that you **are not** disappointed that I **will not** be there. However, maybe **you will** have time to meet me for dinner later. **I will** be free all evening. **Do not** forget to call me so we can make a date.

The Unexpected

HAVEN'T YOU often been surprised by events you couldn't have predicted? Haven't you sometimes been amazed by unexpected revelations about people whom you thought you knew well?

■ The unexpected is a frequent theme in literature. A sudden turn of events makes up the plot of many short stories, but there are usually clues that suggest the outcome. As you read the following stories, look for these clues. How has each author prepared you for the final, unexpected twist?

■ 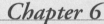 *Chapter 6*

TWO THANKSGIVING DAY GENTLEMEN

– O. Henry

Chapter 4
A Secret for Two QUENTIN REYNOLDS

A PRE-READING

1. Think Before You Read

Answer the following questions:

1. What are some ways animals help human beings?
2. Do you know of any places where horses are used for deliveries of any kind?
3. Why are both French and English spoken in Canada?

2. Picture Focus

With a partner, talk about the picture. What do you think is happening?

3. Story Preview

Read the preview of the story and, with a partner, try to guess the meaning of the words in **bold** print.

The story is set in the first part of the twentieth century in Montreal, Canada, where Pierre Dupin, a milkman, delivers milk by using a horse and **wagon**. Pierre is very fond of his faithful horse, Joseph, who knows the milk **route** as well as Pierre does. The horse is so smart that Pierre says, "I never touch the **reins**. . . . Why, a blind man could handle my route with Joseph pulling the wagon."

For many years, Pierre comes to the **stables** of the Provincale Milk Company every morning and finds Joseph waiting for him. One day, Jacques, Pierre's boss, sees that Pierre is using a cane. Jacques suggests that Pierre may want to stop working. "When Joseph is ready to **retire** – then I, too, will quit," Pierre tells Jacques.

4. Using the Vocabulary

Fill in the blanks below with the **bold** words from the Story Preview above. Then, with a partner, compare your answers.

In the nineteenth and early twentieth centuries in the United States and Canada, it was common to see a horse pulling a _____wagon_____. This is the way fruit, vegetables, milk, and other household items were delivered. The delivery man would sit on top of the wagon and use _____ to control the horse. Horses were also used for transportation. Today, people have garages next to their houses, but in those days many families had _____ for the horses next to their houses. The first "buses" were horses and wagons that picked people up along the same _____ every day.

   Dogs help people, too. They have always been used to guard homes and property. Dogs guide the blind, and they also provide companionship for children and elderly people who _____ from their jobs.

5. Making Predictions

Look at the title of the story and then reread the Story Preview. Which of the following predictions is the most *probable?* Circle your choice or give an answer that you think is better.

1. Pierre and Jacques share a secret.

2. Pierre and Joseph share a secret.

3. Jacques and Joseph share a secret.

4. _____

Journal Writing   In your journal, explain why you chose your answer.

IDIOMS AND EXPRESSIONS	

sing out call out
make out (a bill) prepare *(a bill)*
panic-stricken very frightened
wear out become old and unable to
    work
	take today off not go to work today
	scream of brakes sound of a car
	    stopping suddenly

6. Literary Term: Foreshadowing

If you read mystery stories, you probably look for clues that tell you how the mystery is going to be solved. Do you like to try to figure out who the guilty person is even before you reach the end? In any story of suspense, the author will drop some hints along the way to prepare you for the ending. These hints are called **foreshadowing.**

Focus   As you read "A Secret for Two," look for hints that foreshadow the secret. What is the secret? You may discover it before the end of the story.

About the Author

Quentin Reynolds (1902–1965) was born in New York City and became a newspaper reporter and sportswriter for various New York newspapers. During World War II, *Collier's* magazine sent Reynolds to Europe to serve as a war correspondent. He wrote a book about the conflict entitled *The Wounded Don't Cry.* When the war ended, Reynolds returned to the United States to write articles and short stories for *Collier's.*

■   ■   ■   ■   ■   ■   ■   ■   ■   ■   ■

A Secret for Two

Montreal is a very large city, but, like all large cities, it has some very small streets. Streets, for instance, like Prince
5   Edward Street, which is only four blocks long, ending in a cul de sac.[1] No one knew Prince Edward Street as well as did Pierre Dupin, for Pierre had
10   delivered milk to the families on the street for thirty years now.

During the past fifteen years the horse which drew the milk wagon used by Pierre was a large white horse named
15   Joseph. In Montreal, especially in that part of Montreal which is very French, the animals, like children, are often given the names of saints. When the big white horse first came to the Provincale Milk Company he didn't
20   have a name. They told Pierre that he could use the white horse henceforth. Pierre stroked the softness of the horse's neck; he stroked the sheen of its splendid belly and he looked into the
25   eyes of the horse.

"This is a kind horse, a gentle and a faithful horse," Pierre said, "and I can see a beautiful spirit shining out of the eyes of the horse. I will name him after good
30   St. Joseph, who was also kind and gentle and faithful and a beautiful spirit."

Within a year Joseph knew the milk route as well as Pierre. Pierre used to

---

[1] *cul de sac:* a dead-end street. Literally translated, the French means, "the bottom of a bag."

boast that he didn't need reins – he never touched them. Each morning Pierre arrived at the stables of the Provincale Milk Company at five o'clock. The wagon would be loaded and Joseph hitched to it. Pierre would call *"Bonjour, vieil ami,"*[2] as he climbed into his seat and Joseph would turn his head and the other drivers would smile and say that the horse would smile at Pierre. Then Jacques, the foreman, would say, "All right, Pierre, go on," and Pierre would call softly to Joseph, *"Avance, mon ami,"*[3] and this splendid combination would stalk proudly down the street.

The wagon, without any direction from Pierre, would roll three blocks down St. Catherine Street, then turn right two blocks along Roslyn Avenue; then left, for that was Prince Edward Street. The horse would stop at the first house, allow Pierre perhaps thirty seconds to get down from his seat and put a bottle of milk at the front door and would then go on, skipping two houses and stopping at the third. So down the length of the street. Then Joseph, still without any direction from Pierre, would turn around and come back along the other side. Yes, Joseph was a smart horse.

> ■ ■ ■
>
> *"You should teach that horse to carry the milk to the front door for you,"* *Jacques told him.* *"He does everything else."*
>
> ■ ■ ■

Pierre would boast at the stable of Joseph's skill. "I never touch the reins. He knows just where to stop. Why, a blind man could handle my route with Joseph pulling the wagon."

So it went on for years – always the same. Pierre and Joseph both grew old together, but gradually, not suddenly. Pierre's huge walrus mustache was pure white now and Joseph didn't lift his knees so high or raise his head quite as much. Jacques, the foreman of the stables, never noticed that they were both getting old until Pierre appeared one morning carrying a heavy walking stick.

"Hey, Pierre," Jacques laughed. "Maybe you got the gout, hey?"

"Mais oui, Jacques,"[4] Pierre said a bit uncertainly. "One grows old. One's legs get tired."

"You should teach that horse to carry the milk to the front door for you," Jacques told him. "He does everything else."

He knew every one of the forty families he served on Prince Edward Street. The cooks knew that Pierre could neither read nor write, so instead of following the usual custom of leaving a note in an empty bottle if an additional quart of milk was needed they would sing out when they heard

---

[2] *Bonjour, vieil ami:* Good morning, old friend.
[3] *Avance, mon ami:* Forward, my friend.

[4] *Mais oui, Jacques:* Yes, Jacques; But of course, Jacques.

the rumble of his wagon wheels over the cobbled street, "Bring an extra quart this morning, Pierre."

"So you have company for dinner tonight," he would call back gaily.

Pierre had a remarkable memory. When he arrived at the stable he'd always remember to tell Jacques, "The Paquins took an extra quart this morning; the Lemoines bought a pint of cream."

Jacques would note these things in a little book he always carried. Most of the drivers had to make out the weekly bills and collect the money, but Jacques, liking Pierre, had always excused him from this task. All Pierre had to do was to arrive at five in the morning, walk to his wagon, which was always in the same spot at the curb, and deliver his milk. He returned some two hours later, got down stiffly from his seat, called a cheery *"Au'voir"*[5] to Jacques and then limped slowly down the street.

One morning, the president of the Provincale Milk Company came to inspect the early morning deliveries. Jacques pointed Pierre out to him and said: "Watch how he talks to that horse. See how the horse listens and how he turns his head toward Pierre? See the look in that horse's eyes? You know, I think those two share a secret. I have often noticed it. It is as though they both sometimes chuckle at us as they go off on their route. Pierre is a good man, Monsieur President, but he gets old. Would it be too bold of me to suggest that he be retired and be given perhaps a small pension?" he added anxiously.

"But of course," the president laughed. "I know his record. He has been on this route now for thirty years and never once has there been a complaint. Tell him it is time he rested. His salary will go on just the same."

But Pierre refused to retire. He was panic-stricken at the thought of not driving Joseph every day. "We are two old men," he said to Jacques. "Let us wear out together. When Joseph is ready to retire – then I, too, will quit."

Jacques, who was a kind man, understood. There was something about Pierre and Joseph which made a man smile tenderly. It was as though each drew some hidden strength from the other. When Pierre was sitting in his seat, and when Joseph was hitched to the wagon, neither seemed old. But when they finished their work, then Pierre would limp down the street slowly, seeming very old indeed, and the horse's head would drop and he would walk very wearily to his stall.

Then one morning Jacques had dreadful news for Pierre when he arrived. It was a cold morning and still pitch-dark. The air was like iced wine that morning and the snow which had fallen during the night glistened like a million diamonds piled together.

Jacques said, "Pierre, your horse, Joseph, did not wake up this morning. He was very old, Pierre, he was twenty-five and that is like being seventy-five for a man."

"Yes," Pierre said, slowly. "Yes. I am seventy-five. And I cannot see Joseph again."

[5] *Au'voir* or *Au revoir:* Good-bye; Till we meet again.

"Of course you can," Jacques soothed. "He is over in his stall, looking very peaceful. Go over and see him."

Pierre took one step forward then turned. "No . . . no . . . you don't understand, Jacques."

Jacques clapped him on the shoulder. "We'll find another horse just as good as Joseph. Why, in a month you'll teach him to know your route as well as Joseph did. We'll . . ."

The look in Pierre's eyes stopped him. For years Pierre had worn a heavy cap, the peak of which came low over his eyes, keeping the bitter morning wind out of them. Now Jacques looked into Pierre's eyes and he saw something which startled him. He saw a dead, lifeless look in them. The eyes were mirroring the grief that was in Pierre's heart and his soul. It was as though his heart and soul had died.

"Take today off, Pierre," Jacques said, but already Pierre was hobbling off down the street, and had one been near one would have seen tears streaming down his cheeks and have heard half-smothered sobs. Pierre walked to the corner and stepped into the street. There was a warning yell from the driver of a huge truck that was coming fast and there was the scream of brakes, but Pierre apparently heard neither.

Five minutes later an ambulance driver said, "He's dead. Was killed instantly."

Jacques and several of the milk-wagon drivers had arrived and they looked down at the still figure.

"I couldn't help it," the driver of the truck protested, "he walked right into my truck. He never saw it, I guess. Why, he walked into it as though he were blind."

The ambulance doctor bent down, "Blind? Of course the man was blind. See those cataracts? This man has been blind for five years." He turned to Jacques, "You say he worked for you? Didn't you know he was blind?"

"No . . . no . . ." Jacques said, softly. "None of us knew. Only one knew — a friend of his named Joseph. . . . It was a secret, I think, just between those two."

1. *Understanding the Story*

With a partner, answer these questions.

1. Why does Pierre refuse to retire from the milk company?
2. What does Pierre mean when he says, "I cannot see Joseph again"?
3. Why doesn't Pierre hear the truck driver's warning yell?
4. What is the meaning of the title of the story?

2. *Vocabulary Comprehension*

Choose the word from the following list that best completes each of the sentences below. Do not use the same word more than once.

complaint	stiff	cataracts	limped
loaded	wearily	share	spirit

1. After working all day and studying at the library all evening, I walked

    _____*wearily*_____ home.

2. Everyone cooked something different for the party so that we all could

    _____ the food and try many different things.

3. The store manager was unhappy when a customer made a _____

    about the bad service he had received.

4. The plane couldn't take off until all the baggage was _____.

5. It's always pleasant to be around Julia because she has such a lovely

    _____.

6. Kevin was delighted when his mother's operation for _____ was

    successful and she could see again.

7. The pitcher's arm was so _____ after the baseball game that he

    could hardly move it.

8. After hurting its foot on a stone, the horse _____ back to the stable.

3. Word Forms

Complete the chart by filling in the various forms of the following words taken from "A Secret for Two." An X indicates that no form is possible. Use your dictionary if you need help. **Note:** There may be more than one possible word for the same part of speech.

VERB	NOUN	ADJECTIVE	ADVERB
boast	*boast*		
	complaint	X	
		retired	
limp			
	direction		
load			X
	delivery		X
excuse			X
skip		skippable	X

With a partner, write sentences using *boast*, *limp*, and *excuse* as nouns.

4. Grammar: Prepositions of Place **on, in,** *and* **into**

Prepositions are words that connect nouns or noun phrases. Usually, prepositions show relationships of place, time, or direction.

On **refers to a noun thought of as a line or surface.**

Examples:
Pierre had delivered milk to the families on the street for thirty years now.
"He has been on this route now for thirty years and never once has there been a complaint."
Jacques clapped him on the shoulder.

In refers to a space thought of as being enclosed within boundaries.

Examples:
In Montreal, especially in that part of Montreal which is very French, the animals, like children, are often given the names of saints.
Jacques would note these things in a little book he always carried.

Into is used to express the idea of movement from one place to another.

Examples:
Pierre walked to the corner and stepped into the street.
"I couldn't help it," the driver of the truck protested, "he walked right into my truck."

5. Application

Complete the sentences below with *on, in,* or *into*.

1. Karen parked her car _____on_____ the street in front of the Green Tree Café.

2. Karen put her bag _____ the chair next to her and picked up the menu that was _____ the table.

3. As Karen was trying to decide between espresso and cappuccino, Jennifer arrived _____ her bicycle.

4. Karen and Jennifer had coffee and then decided to sit _____ the park and talk.

5. As Karen and Jennifer talked, children were playing _____ the playground nearby, and there were lots of people _____ the park who were just enjoying the sunny day.

6. Sharon, a co-worker of Karen's, came _____ the park, and they chatted for a while.

7. Then Sharon left and went back to the office. As she was going _____ the elevator, however, she realized she'd left her newspaper _____ the park.

1. Sharing Ideas

Discuss the following questions with a partner or in a group:

1. Discuss the relationship between Pierre and Jacques. How did Jacques feel about Pierre? Find sentences in the story to support your opinion.
2. Do you know any disabled person who depends on an animal?
3. If you ever had a pet, you may have noticed that the animal had some human qualities. Tell your classmates about an incident when your pet seemed to act like a human.

2. Reading Between the Lines

Drawing an inference is another expression for reading between the lines. In mysteries and other stories with surprises, the author may try to prevent you from discovering the surprise by leading you to draw inferences that steer you away from the right conclusion.

Circle the letter of the inference you drew based on the information below. Was it the inference the author wanted you to draw?

1. When Joseph stops at all the right houses, the inference is that
   a. Joseph has learned the route from taking it so many times.
   b. Pierre is giving Joseph a secret signal to stop.
   c. Joseph has human intelligence.

2. When Pierre comes to work carrying a walking stick, the inference is that
   a. he has the gout.
   b. he has lost his sight.
   c. he is having trouble with his legs.

3. The cooks know that Pierre can't read or write, and Jacques excuses Pierre from making out the bills. The inference is that
   a. Pierre doesn't want to be bothered with the details of his job.
   b. Pierre is uneducated.
   c. Pierre can't see very well.

3. Analyzing the Story

Pierre's secret, as you now know, is that he is blind. Look back at the Literary Term on page 48. Did you find all the clues that the author put in the story to foreshadow Pierre's secret? The following three types of clues are used:

1. clues related to Joseph and the wagon
2. clues related to Pierre's appearance, something Pierre says or does, or something the author tells us about Pierre
3. clues related to something Jacques says or does

Make a chart like the one below. Fill in the sentences from the story that provide the clues.

Joseph and the Wagon	Pierre	Jacques
Within a year Joseph knew the milk route as well as Pierre.		

Pair Discussion With a partner, compare what you have written in your charts. Correct any mistakes you find. Then think about when you first realized that Pierre was blind. Did you realize it before the end of the story? If you did, which clue made you guess the secret?

4. Writing

Choose one of the following writing assignments:

1. Write a summary of the story in two to three paragraphs. Make sure to include all of the major events.
2. Imagine you are a reporter and you are called to the scene of the accident. Interview Jacques and the truck driver who accidentally killed Pierre. Write an account for your newspaper.
3. Make up a conversation that might occur between the Paquins and the Lemoines when they hear of Pierre's death.
4. Write about the relationship you have or have had with an animal. Explain how you got the animal and discuss how your relationship developed over time.

Chapter 5
Johanna JANE YOLEN

PRE-READING

1. Think Before You Read

Answer the following questions:

1. Have you ever walked in the woods at night? If so, how did you feel? Were you confident or scared?
2. What are some of the problems wild animals face during the winter?
3. Do you read fairy tales or fantasies? In what ways are they different from realistic stories?

2. Picture Focus

With a partner, talk about the picture. What do you think is happening?

3. Story Preview

Read the preview of the story and, with a partner, try to guess the meaning of the words in **bold** print.

Johanna lived with her mother near Hartwood forest, where **deer** and other animals lived. One winter night, Johanna's mother was so sick that she did not even want the soup made of **acorns** that Johanna usually gathered from the oak trees in the woods and fed to her. So Johanna decided to go through the forest to the village and find the doctor.

Johanna's mother had told her never to go into the forest at night. Her father had once gone into the forest at night and never returned. Johanna had always taken her mother's **warning** seriously, but she decided that she had to make the trip because her mother was just too sick. The story tells about Johanna's journey through the forest.

4. Using the Vocabulary

Fill in the blanks below with the **bold** words from the Story Preview above. Then, with a partner, compare your answers.

In the forests and woods of North America, _____deer_____ are hunted for

their beautiful horns, their skins, and their meat, which has a wild but delicious

taste. These animals are not meat-eaters; rather, they live on plants, berries, and

other vegetarian foods such as _____ from oak trees. Some experts

have recently issued a _____ that certain species of these animals

are dying out, but hunters claim that they mostly hunt other species.

5. Making Predictions

From the Story Preview, try to predict what Johanna is afraid of. Which of the following predictions do you think is the most *probable?* Circle your choice or give an answer that you think is better.

1. Johanna is afraid of wild animals.

2. She is afraid of getting lost.

3. She is afraid of disobeying her mother.

4. She is afraid of the dark.

5. _____

Journal Writing Write in your journal about a time when you were afraid. What did you do to try to overcome your fear?

IDIOMS AND EXPRESSIONS	
grubbed around looked for food on the ground *(meaning in this story)* **hard winter** a cold and snowy winter **maw of the city** the dangerous streets and places of a city *(meaning in this story)*	**gruel** a thin, soup-like cereal **by feel** by using one's hands to guide oneself **a steady tattoo** the sound made by the quick rhythm of feet running on the ground

6. Literary Term: Imagery

In discussions of literature, the term **imagery** refers to the descriptive language that the author uses to paint a picture of the situation, characters, setting, or anything else of importance in the author's story.

Focus As you read "Johanna," try to find any language that gives you a picture of Johanna herself. Look for details about the things she eats, the way she looks, where she lives, the way she moves, and any other information that helps you to visualize the character.

About the Author

Born in New York City, Jane Yolen (1939–) worked for various magazines and publishers in New York before becoming a freelance writer in 1965. She has also been a folk singer, a poet, a playwright, and a teacher. She has won numerous awards for her stories, which include children's stories, fantasies, fairy tales, and science fiction. "Johanna" is taken from her short-story collection entitled *Tales of Wonder*.

Johanna

The forest was dark and the snow-covered path was merely an impression left on Johanna's moccasined feet.

If she had not come this way countless daylit times, Johanna would never have known where to go. But Hartwood[1] was familiar to her, even in the unfamiliar night. She had often picnicked in the cool, shady copses and grubbed around the tall oak trees. In a hard winter like this one, a family could subsist for days on acorn stew.

Still, this was the first night she had ever been out in the forest, though she had lived by it all her life. It was tradition – no, more than that – that members of the Chevril family did not venture into the midnight forest. "Never, never go to the woods at night," her mother said, and it was not a warning so much as a command. "Your father went though he was told not to. He never returned."

And Johanna had obeyed. Her father's disappearance was still in her memory, though she remembered nothing else of him. He was not the first of the Chevrils to go that way. There had been a great-uncle and two girl cousins who had likewise "never returned." At least, that was what Johanna had been told. Whether they had disappeared into the maw of the city that lurked over several mountains to the west, or into the hungry jaws of

---

[1] *Hartwood:* name of forest (Deer Forest).

a wolf or bear, was never made clear. But Johanna, being an obedient girl, always came into the house with the setting sun.

For sixteen years she had listened to that warning. But tonight, with her mother pale and sightless, breathing brokenly in the bed they shared, Johanna had no choice. The doctor, who lived on the other side of the wood, must be fetched. He lived in the cluster of houses that rimmed the far side of Hartwood, a cluster that was known as "the village," though it was really much too small for such a name. The five houses of the Chevril family that clung together, now empty except for Johanna and her mother, were not called a village, though they squatted[2] on as much land.

Usually the doctor himself came through the forest to visit the Chevrils. Once a year he made the trip. Even when the grandparents and uncles and cousins had been alive, the village doctor came only once a year. He was gruff with them and called them "strong as beasts" and went away, never even offering a tonic. They needed none. They were healthy.

But the long, cruel winter had sapped Johanna's mother's strength. She lay for days silent, eyes cloudy and unfocused, barely taking in the acorn gruel that Johanna spooned for her. And at last Johanna had said: "I will fetch the doctor."

Her mother had grunted "no" each day, until this evening. When Johanna mentioned the doctor again, there had been no answering voice. Without her mother's no, Johanna made up her own mind. She *would* go.

If she did not get through the woods and back with the doctor before dawn, she felt it would be too late. Deep inside she knew she should have left before, even when her mother did not want her to go. And so she ran as quickly as she dared, following the small, twisting path through Hartwood by feel.

At first Johanna's guilt and the unfamiliar night were a burden, making her feel heavier than usual. But as she continued running, the crisp night air seemed to clear her head. She felt unnaturally alert, as if she had suddenly begun to discover new senses.

The wind molded her short dark hair to her head. For the first time she felt graceful and light, almost beautiful. Her feet beat a steady tattoo on the snow as she ran, and she felt neither cold nor winded. Her steps lengthened as she went.

Suddenly a broken branch across the path tangled in her legs. She went down heavily on all fours, her breath caught in her throat. As she got to her feet, she searched the darkness ahead. Were there other branches waiting?

Even as she stared, the forest seemed to grow brighter. The light from the full moon must be finding its way into the heart of the woods. It was a comforting thought.

She ran faster now, confident of her steps. The trees seemed to rush by. There would be plenty of time.

[2] *squatted:* lived without permission of the owner.

She came at last to the place where the woods stopped, and cautiously she ranged along the last trees, careful not to be silhouetted against the sky. Then she halted.

She could hear nothing moving, could see nothing that threatened. When she was sure, she edged out onto the short meadow that ran in a downward curve to the back of the village.

Once more she stopped. This time she turned her head to the left and right. She could smell the musk of the farm animals on the wind, blowing faintly up to her. The moon beat down upon her head and, for a moment, seemed to ride on her broad, dark shoulder.

Slowly she paced down the hill toward the line of houses that stood like teeth in a jagged row. Light streamed out of the rear windows, making threatening little earthbound moons on the graying snow.

She hesitated.

A dog barked. Then a second began, only to end his call in a whine.

A voice cried out from the house farthest on the right, a woman's voice, soft and soothing. "Be quiet, Boy."

The dog was silenced.

She dared a few more slow steps toward the village, but her fear seemed to precede her. As if catching its scent, the first dog barked lustily again.

"Boy! Down!" It was a man this time, shattering the night with authority.

She recognized it at once. It was the doctor's voice. She edged toward its sound. Shivering with relief and dread, she came to the backyard of the house on the right and waited. In her nervousness, she moved one foot restlessly, pawing the snow down to the dead grass. She wondered if her father, her great-uncle, her cousins had felt this fear under the burning eye of the moon.

The doctor, short and too stout for his age, come out of the back door, buttoning his breeches with one hand. In the other he carried a gun. He peered out into the darkness.

"Who's there?"

She stepped forward into the yard, into the puddle of light. She tried to speak her name, but she suddenly could not recall it. She tried to tell why she had come, but nothing passed her closed throat. She shook her head to clear the fear away.

The dog barked again, excited, furious.

"By gosh," the doctor said, "it's a deer."

She spun around and looked behind her, following his line of sight. There was nothing there.

"That's enough meat to last the rest of this cruel winter," he said. He raised the gun, and fired.

1. Understanding the Story

With a partner, answer these questions.

1. Why doesn't Johanna's mother want her to go into the forest at night?
2. Why does Johanna disobey her mother?
3. How often does the doctor visit the Chevril family?
4. Does anything bad happen to Johanna in the forest?
5. Who does Johanna encounter when she comes to the houses at the edge of the forest?
6. Why can't Johanna tell the doctor who she is?
7. How does the story end?

2. Vocabulary Comprehension

Choose the word from the following list that best completes each of the sentences below. Do not use the same word more than once.

tradition	obey	pale	unfocused
alert	graceful	threatened	
soothing	precedes	furious	

1. In our family, it is a _____tradition_____ to eat roast duck for Christmas. We do that every year.

2. When someone or something puts you in a dangerous situation, it is natural to feel _____.

3. Johanna was worried that her mother might be angry and even _____ if Johanna disobeyed her.

4. Many large animals, such as deer, are very fast and move in a way that is beautiful and _____.

5. When people go for a walk through the forest for the first time, the leader of the group usually _____ the rest of the people, who follow behind.

6. Some people don't like bright, bold colors; instead, they prefer

   _____ ones.

7. Parents generally want their children to _____ them because

   the rules that parents set for them are most often in the children's best

   interests.

8. People who work very late sometimes start to make a lot of mistakes because

   they are too tired to be _____.

9. The sound of the waves was so _____ that I fell asleep on the

   beach.

10. If you look through a camera and the view is not clear, the camera is

    _____.

3. Word Forms

Complete the chart by filling in the various forms of the following words taken from "Johanna." An X indicates that no form is possible. Use your dictionary if you need help. **Note:** There may be more than one possible word for the same part of speech.

Verb	Noun	Adjective	Adverb
obey	_obedience_	_____	_____
disappear	_____	X	X
feel	_____	_____	_____
comfort	_____	_____	_____
threaten	_____	_____	_____
silence	_____	_____	_____

Work with a partner. Write sentences using some of the word forms above. Write at least one sentence using a noun, one sentence using an adjective, and one sentence using an adverb.

4. Grammar: Articles with Count Nouns

■ Singular count nouns take either *a/an* or *the*. Use *a/an* when information about something is new.

Examples:
I bought a dress yesterday.
A dog barked.

Use *the* when information about something is already known.

Examples:
I'm going to wear the dress this weekend.
(For example, if this is a dress we already know about, such as one I
   bought yesterday.)
The dog was silenced.
(The author has already mentioned the dog.)

■ Literary use of *the:* When an author uses *the* the first time something is mentioned, the author is suggesting that the reader already knows the information. This is a literary technique for making a story more interesting.

Example:
The forest was dark and the snow-covered path was merely an
   impression left on Johanna's moccasined feet.

■ Plural nouns take no article when they refer to something that is new information (when they refer to things that are not yet known or mentioned).

Examples:
She felt unnaturally alert, as if she had suddenly begun to discover new
   senses.
(There is no article because this is the first time the reader hears about
   "new" senses.)
The doctor called the Chevrils "strong as beasts."
(This reference is to beasts in general; these are not specific beasts that
   the reader knows about.)

Plural nouns take *the* when the objects mentioned are already known about (or assumed to be known about).

Example:
The trees seemed to rush by.
(The reader knows Johanna is in the woods, so the reader knows that there are trees in the woods.)

5. Application

Read the sentences from the story and then reread the part of the story that the sentences come from. Explain why the thing referred to in the **bold** words is something that the reader knows about (if *the* is used) or something that the reader does not know about (if *a/an* or no article is used). With a partner, compare your work. The first sentence has been done for you.

1. In **a hard winter** like this one, a family could subsist for days on acorn stew.

   This is the first time the reader learns that the winter is hard.

2. There had been **a great-uncle** and two girl cousins who had likewise "never returned."

3. As if catching its scent, **the first dog** barked lustily again.

4. He lived in the cluster of houses that rimmed the far side of Hartwood, a cluster that was known as "**the village**". . . .

5. In her nervousness, she moved one foot restlessly, pawing **the snow** down to the dead grass.

6. "By gosh," the doctor said, "it's **a deer**."

1. Sharing Ideas

Discuss the following questions with a partner or in a group:

1. Describe Johanna's thoughts as she ran through the forest. How did they change between the time she entered the forest and the time she arrived at the village?
2. What do you think happened to Johanna's father and cousins?
3. Based on what the author tells us about the doctor, how would you describe his character?

2. Reading Between the Lines

Practice reading between the lines. Circle the letter of the answer that best completes each of the following statements:

1. Johanna's mother didn't want her to go into the forest at night because
   a. she might get lost.
   b. she might get eaten by a wolf or a bear.
   c. it's too dark to see in the forest at night.

2. On his yearly visits to Johanna's family, the doctor
   a. gives them medicine.
   b. helps them to find food.
   c. doesn't do anything specific.

3. We can conclude from the author's statements that Johanna
   a. was foolish to disobey her mother.
   b. did not know her way in the forest.
   c. became a target in the moonlight.

3. Analyzing the Story

Johanna's family name is "Chevril." The author took this name from *chevreuil*, the French word for "deer." Much of the imagery in the story slowly puts together a picture of Johanna that is completely revealed only at the end – that she is a deer herself. Look back at the Literary Term on page 60 and think about the images that the author uses to portray Johanna. Make a diagram like the one below, and fill in as many details as you can find. Line numbers are provided as hints.

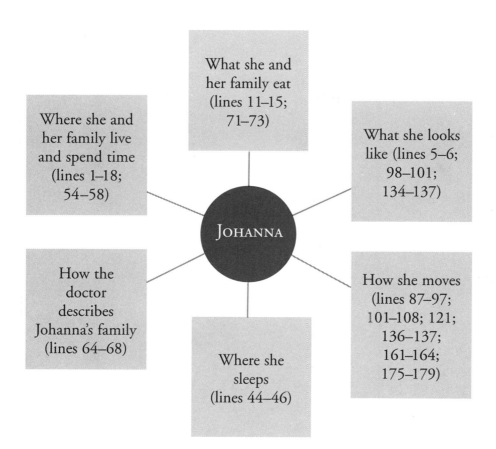

Pair Discussion With a partner, compare what you have written in the boxes. Correct any mistakes you find and discuss your ideas. Are there any other ways the author suggests that Johanna is a deer?

4. Writing

Choose one of the following writing assignments:

1. Write a summary of the story in two to three paragraphs. Be sure to include all of the major events.
2. Write a different ending to this story in two to three paragraphs.
3. Pretend you are the author of this story. Explain your reasons for writing it.
4. Do you think it's all right for humans to kill other animals for food? Write two to three paragraphs about why you think so or don't think so.
5. Do you think hunters should be able to hunt species that are dying out? Write two to three paragraphs about why you think so or don't think so.

Chapter 6

Two Thanksgiving Day Gentlemen O. HENRY

A | PRE-READING

1. *Think Before You Read*

Answer the following questions:

1. What is a tradition? What are some traditions in your family?
2. Do you think traditions are important? Why or why not?
3. What do you know about the American holiday of Thanksgiving?
4. Have you ever pretended to be happy to please someone else? Why or why not?

2. *Picture Focus*

With a partner, talk about the picture. What do you think is happening?

3. Story Preview

Read the preview of the story and, with a partner, try to guess the meaning of the words in **bold** print.

Stuffy Pete is one of the two main characters in "Two Thanksgiving Day Gentlemen." His nickname is "Stuffy" because he **stuffs** himself with food at every opportunity. Unfortunately, he doesn't have many opportunities to do this because he is poor – so poor that he wears torn, **ragged** clothes. For the last nine years, however, the Old Gentleman, the other main character in the story, has taken Stuffy to a restaurant on Thanksgiving Day. The Old Gentleman enjoys paying for Stuffy's dinner and watching Stuffy enjoy his **feast.**

The Old Gentleman is a **philanthropist** who gets pleasure from giving to someone less fortunate than himself. He and Stuffy Pete see each other only on Thanksgiving Day for their traditional dinner. This story is about a Thanksgiving Day that turns out to be unusual for both of them.

4. Using the Vocabulary

Fill in the blanks below with the **bold** words from the Story Preview above. Then, with a partner, compare your answers. Change the form of the word if necessary.

In the United States, it is traditional for a ____philanthropist____ to give food,

clothes, or money to poor people on major holidays, such as Thanksgiving and

Christmas. Churches and community centers serve free dinners for the poor on

those days, too. Sometimes, they put together baskets of clothes so poor people

who have _____ clothes can exchange them for better ones.

A typical Thanksgiving _____ includes soup, roast turkey,

cranberry sauce, potatoes, vegetables, bread, salad, and pumpkin pie for dessert. If

you are a guest at this kind of meal, it is very easy to _____ yourself

with too much food.

5. Making Predictions

Based on the Story Preview, which of the following predictions is the most *probable?* Circle your choice or give an answer that you think is better.

1. The Old Gentleman decides not to take Stuffy to dinner on Thanksgiving Day anymore.

2. Stuffy decides that he doesn't want to accept the Old Gentleman's philanthropy anymore.

3. Stuffy cooks Thanksgiving dinner for the Old Gentleman.

4. _____

Journal Writing   In your journal, explain why you chose your answer.

IDIOMS AND EXPRESSIONS	
lick 'em defeat them, beat them **took his seat** sat down **stared into space** looked at nothing in particular; was unaware of what was happening around him; daydreamed	**music in his ears** something he was happy to hear **treats** pays for **didn't have the heart to** didn't want to

6. Literary Term: Theme

A story's **theme** is the main idea that runs through the narrative. Sometimes, a story has several themes.

Focus   One of the themes in "Two Thanksgiving Day Gentlemen" is respect for tradition. As you read, ask yourself how Stuffy Pete and the Old Gentleman each show that they respect the tradition of Thanksgiving.

About the Author

O. Henry's real name was William Sydney Porter (1862–1910), but he used the pen name O. Henry. Although he is best known for his stories about New York City, he didn't actually live in New York until 1902. Born and raised in North Carolina, he moved to Texas in 1882. While in Texas, he wrote stories but also worked in a bank to support his wife and child. He was accused and convicted of stealing money from the bank and served three years in prison. During his prison term, he developed his writing technique. From fellow prisoners he heard some of the interesting stories that he used in his work.

After O. Henry moved to New York and began to make his living as a short-story writer, he continued to be fascinated with down-and-out people. The colorful characters he met in the streets and cafés of the city became immortalized in his stories. "Two Thanksgiving Day Gentlemen" deals with two such characters. O. Henry was the first American writer to popularize the surprise ending, another feature of the story you are about to read.

Two Thanksgiving Day Gentlemen

There is one day that is ours. There is one day when all Americans like to go back home to eat a big dinner and feel they are part of a family. Bless the day. We hear some talk about the Puritans and the original Thanksgiving. But that was a long time ago. They landed on Plymouth Rock in Massachusetts after escaping religious persecution in England. I'll bet we could lick 'em if they tried to land again today.

They were lucky. The Indians they met took pity on them and helped them survive the winter. The first feast was held to celebrate their survival and their friendship with the original

Americans, the Indians. Today we celebrate the fourth Thursday in November as a national holiday. It is one day that is purely American. Yes, it is a day of celebration, exclusively American.

The following story will prove to you that we have traditions on this side of the ocean even though we are still a young country. Our story takes place in New York City on Thanksgiving Day.

Stuffy Pete took his seat on the third bench to the right as you enter Union Square from the east, at the walk opposite the fountain. Every Thanksgiving Day for nine years he had taken his seat there promptly at one o'clock. For every time he had done so, he had been rewarded with a feast.

But today Stuffy Pete's appearance at the annual meeting place was a result of habit rather than hunger – which philanthropists seem to think the poor feel only on holidays. It seems that these are the only times the well-fed think of their less fortunate brothers and sisters.

Stuffy Pete was not hungry. He had just come from a feast that left him barely able to breathe and move about. His breath came in short wheezes. The buttons that had been sewn on his coat by Salvation Army workers were popping from the pressure of his fat belly. His clothes were ragged and his shirt was split open. The November breeze, carrying fine snowflakes, brought a grateful coolness. Stuffy Pete was still recovering from a huge dinner beginning with oysters and ending with plum pudding and including (it seemed to him) all the roast turkey and baked potatoes and chicken salad and squash pie and ice cream in the world.

The meal had been an unexpected one. He was passing a red brick mansion near the beginning of Fifth Avenue. In this mansion there lived two old ladies of a traditional family. One of their traditional habits was to station a servant at the gate with orders to admit the first hungry person who walked by after the hour of noon. Stuffy happened to pass by on his way to Union Square and the servants upheld their custom.

Our story takes place in New York City on Thanksgiving Day.

After stuffing himself and confirming the meaning of his name, Stuffy wandered on to the square as he had done so many times before. He sat on the park bench for ten minutes and stared into space. With a tremendous effort he turned his head slowly to the left. His eyes bulged out and his breath ceased. The Old Gentleman was coming across the walk toward his bench.

Every Thanksgiving Day for nine years the Old Gentleman had come there and found Stuffy Pete on the bench. Every Thanksgiving Day for nine years he had led Stuffy Pete to a restaurant and watched him eat a big dinner. The Old Gentleman was a proud American patriot, and he was pleased to have established this Thanksgiving Day tradition with Stuffy Pete. It was extremely important to the Old Gentleman that their tradition should continue.

The annual feeding of Stuffy Pete was significant. It showed, at least, that traditions were possible not only in England. They were possible in America, too!

The Old Gentleman was thin and tall and sixty. He was dressed all in black and wore the old-fashioned kind of glasses that won't stay on your nose. His hair was whiter and thinner than it had been last year, and he seemed to make more use of his big, knobby cane with the crooked handle.

As his benefactor came up, Stuffy Pete wheezed and shuddered like some over-fat pug when a street dog snarls at him. He would have escaped, but he was too full to move quickly.

"Good afternoon," said the Old Gentleman. "I am glad to see that this year you are enjoying good health in the beautiful world. For that blessing alone this day of thanksgiving is well proclaimed to each of us. If you will come with me, my man, I will provide you with a dinner that will satisfy you physically and mentally."

That is what the Old Gentleman had said every time on every Thanksgiving Day for nine years. Nothing compared with these words except the Declaration of Independence. Always before they had been music in Stuffy's ears. But now he looked up at the Old Gentleman's face with tearful agony. The Old Gentleman shivered a little and turned his back to the wind.

Stuffy had always wondered why the Old Gentleman spoke his speech a little sadly. He did not know that it was because he was wishing every time that he had a son to succeed him. A son who would come there after he was gone – a son who would stand proud and strong before some future Stuffy and say: "In memory of my father." Then the tradition would be an institution.

But the Old Gentleman had no relatives. He lived in rented rooms in one of the decayed old family brownstone mansions on one of the quiet streets east of the park. In the winter he raised fuschias in a little greenhouse the size of a closet. In the spring he walked in the Easter Parade. In the summer he lived in a farmhouse in the New Jersey hills, and sat in a wicker armchair, speaking of a rare butterfly that he hoped to find some day. In the autumn he fed Stuffy a dinner. These were the Old Gentleman's occupations.

Stuffy looked at him. The Old Gentleman's eyes were bright with the pleasure of giving. His face was getting more lined each year, but his black necktie was in a bow, his shirt was beautiful and white, and his gray mustache was curled gracefully at the ends.

"Thank you, sir. I'll go with you and I'm very grateful. I'm very hungry, sir," said Stuffy Pete. His Thanksgiving appetite was not his own; it belonged by established custom to this kind, old gentleman. True, America is free. It got this freedom through the hard work of its heroes. Though he wasn't as famous as George Washington or Abraham Lincoln, Stuffy Pete was a hero who fought bravely to maintain tradition.

The Old Gentleman led his guest to the restaurant and to the table where the feast had always been served. They were recognized by the waiters. "Here comes that old guy who always treats that same bum to a meal every Thanksgiving."

The Old Gentleman sat across the table glowing with the pride one feels after doing a good deed. The waiters covered the table with holiday food and Stuffy began eating.

Our valiant hero fought his way through turkey, chops, soups, vegetables, and pies. Every time he felt discouraged and ready to give up the battle, he looked at the Old Gentleman. He saw the look of happiness on the Old Gentleman's face, and it gave him the courage to go on. Stuffy did not have the heart to see the Old Gentleman's happiness wane. In an hour Stuffy leaned back with the battle won.

"Thank you kindly, sir. Thank you kindly for a hearty meal," Stuffy said. Then he got up with glazed eyes and started toward the kitchen. A waiter turned him around and pointed toward the door. The Old Gentleman carefully counted out $1.30 in change, leaving three dimes for the waiter.

They parted as they did every year at the door, the Old Gentleman going south, Stuffy going north.

Stuffy turned around the first corner and stood for one minute. Then he seemed to puff out his rags as an owl puffs out its feathers, and fell to the sidewalk like a horse who has been in the sun too long.

When the ambulance came the young doctor and the driver cursed at his weight. Stuffy did not smell from whiskey, so instead of transferring him to the police, Stuffy and his two dinners went to the hospital. There they stretched him on a bed and started testing him for strange diseases.

An hour later another ambulance brought the Old Gentleman. They laid him on another bed and talked about his case. Pretty soon one of the young doctors met one of the young nurses, whose eyes he liked, and stopped to chat with her about the cases.

"That nice old gentleman over there, now," he said. "You wouldn't think that was a case of near starvation. Proud old family, I guess. He told me he hadn't eaten a thing in three days."

1. Understanding the Story

With a partner, answer these questions.

1. Where does Stuffy Pete have his first Thanksgiving dinner? What does he eat?
2. What tradition do Stuffy Pete and the Old Gentleman maintain? For how many years have they maintained it?
3. Why is Stuffy Pete taken to the hospital?
4. Why is the Old Gentleman taken to the hospital?

2. Vocabulary Comprehension

Match each vocabulary word in the left column with the correct definition on the right. Write the letter of the definition in the space provided.

_c_	1. wheeze	a. brave
	2. proud	b. stopped
	3. annual	c. breathe with difficulty
	4. split	d. weakness or death due to lack of food
	5. feast	e. fill something too full
	6. shiver	f. old and not in good shape
	7. starvation	g. large, luxurious home
	8. valiant	h. stuck out; pushed out
	9. wane	i. divided into two or more parts
	10. ceased	j. shake because of feeling cold
	11. patriot	k. torn and in bad condition
	12. ragged	l. a person who loves his or her country
	13. decayed	m. large, delicious meal
	14. bulged	n. once a year
	15. stuff	o. weaken
	16. mansion	p. feeling satisfaction for something you possess or have achieved

3. Word Forms

Complete the chart by filling in the various forms of the following words taken from "Two Thanksgiving Day Gentlemen." An X indicates that no form is possible. Use your dictionary if you need help. **Note:** There may be more than one possible word for the same part of speech.

VERB	NOUN	ADJECTIVE	ADVERB
X	tradition	_traditional_	_____
X	_____	proud	_____
shiver	_____	_____	X
_____	starvation	_____	X
discourage	_____	_____	_____

Work with a partner. Write sentences using a verb, a noun, an adjective, and an adverb from the chart above.

4. Grammar: Agreement of Subject and Verb

The following rules will help you identify the subject and the verb that corresponds to it.

A singular subject takes a singular verb form.
A plural subject takes a plural verb form.

Examples:

Stuffy Pete <u>meets</u> the Old Gentleman every Thanksgiving Day.

subject: Stuffy Pete (singular)
verb: meets (singular form of *meet*)

The two men <u>meet</u> every year on Thanksgiving Day.

    subject: men (plural)
    verb: meet (plural form of *meet*)

A compound subject is a subject with two or more nouns connected by *and*. A compound subject takes a plural verb form.

Example:

Stuffy Pete and the Old Gentleman <u>meet</u> every year.

    subject: Stuffy Pete + and + the Old Gentleman (compound)
    verb: meet (plural form of *meet*)

If a prepositional phrase follows the subject, be careful not to confuse the subject noun with the noun that is the object of the preposition.

Example:

The ladies in the red brick mansion <u>feed</u> poor people.

    subject: ladies (plural)
    prepositional phrase: in the red brick mansion
        preposition: in
        object of the preposition: mansion (singular)
    verb: feed (plural form of *feed;* agrees with *ladies,* not *mansion*)

The phrase *one of* is followed by a plural noun, but it takes a singular verb.

Example:

One of the old ladies' traditional habits <u>was</u> to feed poor people.
    subject: one (singular)
    verb: was (singular form of *be;* agrees with *one*)

5. Application

Practice finding the subject and verb in the following sentences. First, draw an arrow from the subject to the verb. Then circle *singular* or *plural* to describe the subject and verb.

1. They were lucky.

    singular   (plural)

2. Our story takes place in New York City on Thanksgiving Day.

    singular   plural

3. Stuffy Pete's appearance at the annual meeting place was a result of habit rather than hunger. . . .

    singular   plural

4. The buttons on his coat pop off from the pressure of his fat belly.

    singular   plural

5. A waiter with a tray of turkey, chops, soups, vegetables, and pies walks toward their table.

    singular   plural

6. One of the young doctors stops to chat with one of the young nurses.

    singular   plural

Editing Practice   Edit the following paragraph by changing the form of the verb from singular to plural or from plural to singular if necessary:

Our Thanksgiving tradition is to have dinner at home. My mother and father shops for a turkey the weekend before the holiday. Both of them likes to cook, and my sister and I helps them. On Thanksgiving, we all get up early and begin to prepare the food and set the table. We usually sit down to eat about 2 o'clock. After the meal, my brother help with the dishes, and my sister come with me for a walk.

D | THINKING ABOUT THE STORY

1. Sharing Ideas

Discuss the following questions with a partner or in a group:

1. How do you feel about Stuffy Pete when you first meet him in the story?
2. How do you feel about him at the end of the story?
3. There is only one character in the story called a "gentleman," but the title of the story is "*Two* Thanksgiving Day Gentlemen." Why does O. Henry use the word "two" in the story's title?
4. There is a saying, "You can't judge a book by its cover." How does it apply to the story you have just read?

2. Reading Between the Lines

Practice reading between the lines. Circle the letter of each correct conclusion from among the following statements:

1. "We hear some talk about the Puritans and the original Thanksgiving. But that was a long time ago." In these sentences O. Henry is saying that
   a. the first Thanksgiving was a very long time ago.
   b. the Puritans didn't have anything to do with the first Thanksgiving.
   c. the original Thanksgiving was a happy occasion for the Puritans.
   d. most people don't remember the meaning of the first Thanksgiving.

2. When O. Henry says that the story "will prove to you that we have traditions on this side of the ocean even though we are still a young country," he means that
   a. the United States has many traditions.
   b. the United States is a younger country than England, but it has traditions.
   c. England doesn't have traditions.
   d. the United States and England both celebrate Thanksgiving Day.

3. Philanthropists seem to think that the poor only get hungry on holidays because
   a. poor people don't get hungry on other days.
   b. poor people only eat in restaurants on holidays.
   c. rich people usually forget about the poor except on holidays.
   d. poor people walk around looking hungry on holidays.

3. Analyzing the Story

Look back at the Literary Term on page 72. One of the story's themes is the importance of tradition. Both Stuffy Pete and the Old Gentleman respect tradition; yet their ways of doing so are often different. Find as many similarities and differences as you can and write them in the chart below. An example has been provided for you.

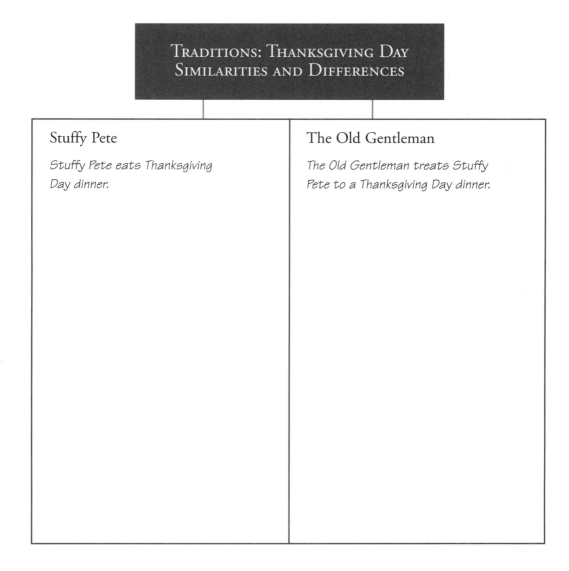

TRADITIONS: THANKSGIVING DAY SIMILARITIES AND DIFFERENCES

Stuffy Pete	The Old Gentleman
Stuffy Pete eats Thanksgiving Day dinner.	*The Old Gentleman treats Stuffy Pete to a Thanksgiving Day dinner.*

Pair Discussion With a partner, compare what you have written in your charts. Correct any mistakes you find. Then discuss the ways Stuffy Pete and the Old Gentleman are similar and different.

4. Writing

Choose one of the following writing assignments:

1. Write a summary of the story in two to three paragraphs. Be sure to include all of the major events.
2. Imagine that you are Stuffy Pete. Write about your thoughts the next day when you wake up in the hospital.
3. Imagine that you are the Old Gentleman. Write about your thoughts when you wake up the next morning in the hospital.
4. Imagine that you are the doctor at the hospital. Describe the two patients – the Old Gentleman and Stuffy Pete.
5. Continue the story a year later. What has happened to Stuffy Pete? What has happened to the Old Gentleman?
6. You are a reporter. Make a list of questions to ask Stuffy Pete and the Old Gentleman about their relationship over the past nine years. You can ask two of your classmates to take the roles of the characters.
7. Write the story in the present time in a different city. Change the characters to two women who meet in a park. You can change details of the story, but don't change the main idea or theme.

Summing Up

A | TAKE A CLOSER LOOK

1. Theme Comparison: Unpredictable Events

In each of the stories in Part Two, something unpredictable happens to one of the characters.

1. What is the unpredictable event in each story?
2. Could any of these three events have been avoided? If so, how?

2. Freewriting

Write the word *unpredictable* on the top of a sheet of paper. Now write any words that come into your mind when you think of this word. For fifteen minutes, write about a time in your life when something unpredictable happened. What was it? What other things happened as a result of this unpredictable event?

B | REVIEW

1. Idioms and Expressions Review

The following story will use some of the idioms you learned in Part Two. Work with a partner or in a small group. Fill in the blanks with the correct idioms and expressions. The first letter of each answer is supplied.

make out	hard winter
doesn't have the heart to	music in his ears

Yesterday, when Bill suggested to Peter that they go camping in the woods today,

it was m_____ _____ _____ _____. Bill and Peter used to camp

together when they were teenagers. They would m_____ _____ a list of all the equipment they needed and head for the woods. Now, after a h_____

_____ , it's early April and they look forward to getting away.

When they reach a deep part of the woods, they hear a strange sound. Bill

turns his head and sees a large shape that looks like a bear. The animal runs off

through the trees. "What is it?" Peter asks. "Oh, nothing," Bill replies. For the rest

of the day, Peter keeps asking about the strange sound. But Bill d_____

_____ _____ _____ _____ tell Peter the truth.

2. *Form Review*

Circle the subject of each verb below. Then, decide if the subject is singular or
plural and write the correct form of the verb in the blank. Use the present tense.

1. Joseph, Pierre's kind, gentle horse, _____ (help) him deliver the milk.

   Joseph and Pierre _____ (go) from house to house each morning, and

   Joseph _____ (know) the route by heart. He and Pierre _____ (be)

   very fond of each other. Jacques and the president of the Provincale Milk

   Company _____ (think) that Pierre _____ (want) to retire. But they

   _____ (not, understand) the special relationship between Joseph and Pierre.

2. The disappearance of Johanna's relatives in the woods _____ (make) her

   respect her mother's command. But when her mother _____ (become)

   deathly ill, Johanna _____ (decide) to disobey her mother and go for the

   doctor. As Johanna _____ (come) out of the woods, one of the dogs

   _____ (bark). When she _____ (reach) the doctor's house, his dog and

   his gun _____ (frighten) her.

3. All the stories in Part Two _____ (have) surprise endings. Surprise endings

   _____ (be) a very popular feature in short stories. One of the authors most

   famous for using them _____ (be) O. Henry, but many other authors also

   _____ (use) them.

PART THREE

Traveling Through Time

THE FUN THEY HAD
– Isaac Asimov

PEOPLE ARE naturally curious about other places and times. Early explorers searched for new lands, and astronauts today travel through space to study our universe. Fiction writers also enjoy exploring space and time. Of course, they can travel with their pens – or computers.

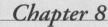 One of the stories that follows is set in the future. The other story involves a contemporary woman who has an extraordinary experience with time. As you read, think about whether you would like to have the same opportunities as the characters in the stories.

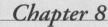 *Chapter 8*

THE MIRROR
– Judith Kay

Chapter 7

The Fun They Had ISAAC ASIMOV

A | PRE-READING

1. Think Before You Read

Answer the following questions:

1. What do you like about school the way it is now? What don't you like about it?
2. Would you like to study without going to a school? Explain your answer.
3. Do you think it is possible to learn without reading books? Explain your answer.
4. What do you think education – schools, teachers, and so on – will be like 150 years in the future?

2. Picture Focus

With a partner, talk about the picture. What do you think is happening?

3. Story Preview

Read the preview of the story and, with a partner, try to guess the meaning of the words in **bold** print.

One day in 2155, Margie's friend Tommy finds a very old book. Tommy and Margie have read many telebooks, but they have never seen a printed book. Although Tommy is reading the book with interest, Margie is **scornful** of the book, especially when she finds out that it is about school. Margie hates school. She especially hates her **mechanical** teacher, which is **geared** to progress at the speed that's right for Margie and which can **calculate** how well she's done on a test almost as soon as she's completed it. Tommy explains that the book is about school in the old days: Children went to school together, instead of each child going to a schoolroom in his or her house. When Margie hears this, she becomes more interested.

4. Using the Vocabulary

Fill in the blanks below with the **bold** words from the Story Preview above. Then, with a partner, compare your answers.

Some people feel that education can be greatly improved if we allow

_____mechanical_____ aids like computers and videos to perform some of the work

that teachers now do. For example, they feel that this way education can be

_____ to the particular needs of each child. They also feel that it is

possible, with computers, to _____ grades in a way that is fair to

everyone. Others, however, are _____ of these ideas. They think it

is wrong and foolish to believe that computers and videos can take the place of

teachers.

5. Making Predictions

From the Story Preview, what do you think the title of the story means? Which of the following predictions is the most *probable?* Circle your choice or give an answer that you think is better.

1. Tommy and Margie had fun reading telebooks.

2. Tommy and Margie had fun reading old books.

3. Tommy and Margie had fun at school.

4. Children in 2155 had fun at school.

5. _____

Journal Writing In your journal, explain why you made your prediction.

IDIOMS AND EXPRESSIONS	
what a waste an unnecessary or impractical use of money, time, or something else **through** *(with)* finished *(with)* **all right** (adv) without a doubt	**made** *(someone do something)* forced or caused *(someone to do something)* **I betcha** I'll bet you *(said when you're quite sure you are right)*

6. Literary Term: Dialogue

When you read a play, you learn about its plot, or story, mainly from the **dialogue** that takes place among the characters – that is, from the characters' conversations. In short stories, although authors can also use narration (tell the story directly), dialogue usually remains important. To be effective, dialogue must be natural and must seem appropriate for the particular characters.

Focus As you read "The Fun They Had," ask yourself if the dialogue, especially between the two children, helped tell the story and if it seemed natural and appropriate for the characters.

About the Author

Isaac Asimov (1920–1992) had a remarkable career as a scientist, teacher, and author. Born in Petrovichi, Russia, Asimov immigrated to the United States, earned a Ph.D. at Columbia University, and taught biochemistry. Although English was not his native language, Asimov wrote nearly 500 books on a variety of subjects, both fiction and nonfiction. His nonfiction work includes *Asimov's Biographical Encyclopedia of Science and Technology*. However, he is most famous for his science fiction stories such as "The Fun They Had," a look into the classrooms of the future.

The Fun They Had

Margie even wrote about it that night in her diary. On the page headed May 17, 2155, she wrote, "Today
5   Tommy found a real book!"

It was a very old book. Margie's grandfather once said that when he was a little boy *his* grandfather told him
10 that there was a time when all stories were printed on paper.

They turned the pages, which were yellow and crinkly, and it was awfully funny to read words that stood still
15 instead of moving the way they were supposed to – on a screen, you know. And then, when they turned back to the page before, it had the same words on it that it had had when they read it the first time.   20

"Gee," said Tommy, "what a waste. When you're through with the book, you just throw it away, I guess. Our television screen must have had a million books on it and it's good for   25 plenty more. I wouldn't throw *it* away."

"Same with mine," said Margie. She was eleven and hadn't seen as many telebooks as Tommy had. He was thirteen.   30

She said, "Where did you find it?"

"In my house." He pointed without looking, because he was busy reading. "In the attic."

"What's it about?"   35
"School."

Margie was scornful. "School? What's there to write about school? I hate school." Margie always hated school, but now she hated it more than ever. The mechanical teacher had been giving her test after test in geography and she had been doing worse and worse until her mother had shaken her head sorrowfully and sent for the County Inspector.

He was a round little man with a red face and a whole box of tools with dials and wires. He smiled at her and gave her an apple, then took the teacher apart. Margie had hoped he wouldn't know how to put it together again, but he knew how all right and, after an hour or so, there it was again, large and black and ugly with a big screen on which all the lessons were shown and the questions were asked. That wasn't so bad. The part she hated most was the slot where she had to put homework and test papers. She always had to write them out in a punch code they made her learn when she was six years old, and the mechanical teacher calculated the mark in no time.

The inspector had smiled after he was finished and patted her head. He said to her mother, "It's not the little girl's fault, Mrs. Jones. I think the geography sector was geared a little too quick. Those things happen sometimes. I've slowed it up to an average ten-year level. Actually, the overall pattern of her progress is quite satisfactory." And he patted Margie's head again.

Margie was disappointed. She had been hoping they would take the teacher away altogether. They had once taken Tommy's teacher away for nearly a month because the history sector had blanked out completely.

So she said to Tommy, "Why would anyone write about school?"

Tommy looked at her with very superior eyes. "Because it's not our kind of school, stupid. This is the old kind of school that they had hundreds and hundreds of years ago." He added loftily, pronouncing the word carefully, "*Centuries* ago."

Margie was hurt. "Well, I don't know what kind of school they had all that time ago." She read the book over his shoulder for a while, then said, "Anyway, they had a teacher."

"Sure they had a teacher, but it wasn't a *regular* teacher. It was a man."

"A man? How could a man be a teacher?"

"Well, he just told the boys and girls things and gave them homework and asked them questions."

"A man isn't smart enough."

"Sure he is. My father knows as much as my teacher."

"He can't. A man can't know as much as a teacher."

"He knows almost as much, I betcha."

Margie wasn't prepared to dispute that. She said, "I wouldn't want a strange man in my house to teach me."

Tommy screamed with laughter, "You don't know much, Margie. The teachers didn't live in the house. They had a special building and all the kids went there."

"And all the kids learned the same thing?"

"Sure, if they were the same age."

"But my mother says a teacher has

to be adjusted to fit the mind of each boy and girl it teaches and that each kid has to be taught differently."

125 "Just the same, they didn't do it that way then. If you don't like it, you don't have to read the book."

"I didn't say I didn't like it," Margie said quickly. She wanted to read about those funny schools.

130 They weren't even half finished when Margie's mother called, "Margie! School!"

Margie looked up. "Not yet, mamma."

135 "Now," said Mrs. Jones. "And it's probably time for Tommy, too."

Margie said to Tommy, "Can I read the book some more with you after school?"

140 "Maybe," he said, nonchalantly. He walked away whistling, the dusty old book tucked beneath his arm.

Margie went into the schoolroom. It was right next to her bedroom, and the

145 mechanical teacher was on and waiting for her. It was always on at the same time every day except Saturday and Sunday, because her mother said little girls learned better if they learned at regular hours.

150 The screen was lit up, and it said: "Today's arithmetic lesson is on the addition of proper fractions. Please insert yesterday's homework in the proper slot."

155 Margie did so with a sigh. She was thinking about the old schools they had when her grandfather's grandfather was a little boy. All the kids from the whole neighborhood came, laughing

160 and shouting in the schoolyard, sitting together in the schoolroom, going home together at the end of the day. They learned the same things so they could help one another on the

165 homework and talk about it.

And the teachers were people. . . .

The mechanical teacher was flashing on the screen: "When we add the fractions ½ and ¼ . . ."

170 Margie was thinking about how the kids must have loved it in the old days. She was thinking about the fun they had.

1. *Understanding the Story*

With a partner, answer these questions.

1. When does this story take place?
2. How is the book that Tommy found different from the books that Margie and Tommy are familiar with? What is it about?
3. How do students in Margie and Tommy's time learn? Where do they go to school? Who are their teachers?
4. How does Margie feel about school? Why?
5. Why does the County Inspector visit Margie's house?
6. What does Margie hope will happen when the County Inspector visits? What does happen?
7. At the beginning of the story, what is Margie's attitude toward the book Tommy found? What is her attitude at the end of the story?

2. *Vocabulary Comprehension*

Read each of the following sentences from the story. Then circle the letter of the correct meaning for each word in **bold** print.

1. Margie even wrote about it that night in her **diary.**
   a. a place for writing down your experiences each day
   b. a place for writing down homework assignments
   c. a file for completed homework and tests
   d. a list of things you need to do or remember

2. They turned the pages, which were yellow and **crinkly**. . . .
   a. bright
   b. curled, not smooth
   c. clear and easy to read
   d. torn into small pieces

3. "[I found it] In my house." He pointed without looking. . . . "In the **attic.**"
   a. an area above the top floor of a house, often used for storage
   b. a part of the house where the family spends a lot of time
   c. a front or back yard of a house
   d. a large bookcase

4. Margie was **scornful.** "School? What's there to write about school? I hate school."
   a. expressing friendliness and understanding
   b. expressing excitement and interest
   c. expressing dislike and lack of respect
   d. expressing great sadness

5. She always had to write [her answers] out in a punch code . . . and the mechanical teacher **calculated** the mark in no time.
   a. guessed the answers
   b. figured out the grade
   c. wrote comments
   d. read the answers

6. "I think the geography **sector** was geared a little too quick."
   a. teacher
   b. part
   c. test
   d. map

7. "I think the geography sector was **geared** a little too quick."
   a. set
   b. broken
   c. prepared
   d. finished

8. Tommy looked at her with very superior eyes. "Because it's not our kind of school, stupid. This is the old kind of school that they had hundreds and hundreds of years ago." He added **loftily** . . . "*Centuries* ago."
   a. as if angry at someone else
   b. as if better than someone else
   c. as if not sure about something
   d. as if in a hurry to leave

9. "[My father] knows almost as much [as my teacher] I betcha." Margie wasn't prepared to **dispute** that. She said, "I wouldn't want a strange man in my house to teach me."
   a. argue about
   b. repeat
   c. laugh at
   d. hear

3. Word Forms

Complete the chart by filling in the various forms of the following words taken from "The Fun They Had." An X indicates that no form is possible. Use your dictionary if you need help. **Note:** There may be more than one possible word for the same part of speech.

VERB	NOUN	ADJECTIVE	ADVERB
write	_writing_	_____	X
_____	_____	mechanical	_____
learn	_____	_____	X
_____	progress	_____	_____
_____	_____	disappointed	_____
hope	_____	_____	_____
_____	_____	_____	completely
_____	_____	special	_____
think	_____	_____	_____

Work with a partner. Write a story about the future using at least eight words from the chart.

4. Grammar: Pronouns, Possessives, Demonstratives

The subject pronouns are *I, you, he, she, it, we,* and *they.* They occur in subject position.

Example:
He was a round little man with a red face. . . .

The object pronouns are *me, you, him, her, it, us,* and *them.* They occur as objects of verbs and of prepositions.

Example:
He smiled at her and gave her an apple. . . .

The possessive pronouns are *mine, yours, his, hers, ours,* and *theirs.* They show possession by taking the place of a noun. The possessive adjectives are *my, your, her, his, its, our, your,* and *their.* They are used with a noun to show possession.

> *Example:*
> "Same with **mine.**" *or* The same with **my** television screen.

The demonstratives are *this, that, these,* and *those.* Demonstratives point to or identify things being talked about. Demonstratives may be used alone as pronouns or with a noun as adjectives.

> *Example:*
> **That** wasn't so bad.
> "**Those** things happen sometimes."

5. Application

The following sentences are from the story. Complete the sentences with the correct subject and object pronouns, possessives, and demonstratives. Then, with a partner, choose a long paragraph from the story and rewrite the paragraph by replacing as many pronouns as possible with the appropriate nouns. Why are pronouns important in writing?

1. Margie even wrote about it ___that___ night in ___her___ diary.

2. Margie's grandfather once said that when _____ was a little boy _____ grandfather told _____ that there was a time when all stories were printed on paper.

3. Margie always hated school, but now _____ hated _____ more than ever.

4. Margie said to Tommy, "Can _____ read the book some more with _____ after school?"

1. Sharing Ideas

Discuss the following questions with a partner or in a group:

1. Would you want to learn the way Margie and Tommy do? Explain.
2. Do you think the way Margie and Tommy learn would be better for some students than the way we learn now? Why or why not?
3. How do you think telebooks work? Would you like to read telebooks instead of regular books? Explain.

2. Reading Between the Lines

Practice reading between the lines. Circle the letter of the answer that best completes each of the following statements:

1. Margie would be most likely to describe her school experience as
   a. stressful and lonely.
   b. too easy and unchallenging.
   c. interesting but too unpredictable.
   d. important to her future.

2. When Margie asks Tommy if they can read the book together after school, he answers "Maybe," rather than "Yes," because
   a. he isn't sure yet about his after-school plans.
   b. he feels angry at Margie because of what she was saying.
   c. now that she's become interested in the book, he wants to tease her.
   d. he's probably going to finish the book before then.

3. It is possible to conclude from the story that, compared to schooling today,
   a. Margie and Tommy's schooling involves more subjects.
   b. Their schooling involves more homework and tests.
   c. Their schooling involves more hours of class time.
   d. Their schooling is more predictable.

3. Analyzing the Story

Look back at the Literary Term on page 90. The plot of "The Fun They Had" becomes clear through the dialogue. The following lines of dialogue come from conversations between Margie and Tommy at four points in the story:

"What's there to write about school?"

"Maybe."

"This is the old kind of school that they had hundreds and hundreds of years ago."

"Well, I don't know what kind of school they had all that time ago."

"They had a special building and all the kids went there."

"What's it about?"

"Can I read the book some more with you after school?"

"School."

"And all the kids learned the same thing?"

"Sure, if they were the same age."

Make a chart like the one below. Decide at which point in the story these lines of dialogue occur. Then complete the first two columns of your chart. The first line of dialogue has been done for you.

Margie	Tommy	Plot (Margie's attitude toward the book and school in the old days)
1. *"What's it about?"*		
2.		
3.		
4.		

Pair Discussion   Compare charts with a partner. Correct any mistakes you find. Then, together, complete the third column. Do you think the dialogue is effective in telling the story? Do you think it is natural? Why or why not?

4. Writing

Choose one of the following writing assignments:

1. Write a summary of the story in two to three paragraphs. Be sure to include all of the major events. Look at your chart for Analyzing the Story if you need help.
2. Write a dialogue between Margie and her mother, in which Margie tells her mother about the book and the schools described in it. How does her mother respond? What is Margie's reaction?
3. If you could design a system of education, what would this system be like? Describe the kind of school you think would be best.

Chapter 8
The Mirror JUDITH KAY

A | PRE-READING

1. Think Before You Read

Answer the following questions:

1. How important are youth and beauty in your country? For example, how important are these qualities in movies and advertising?
2. How do people who are not young or beautiful feel about the importance of youth and beauty?
3. Have you ever wanted to be like someone else who was very beautiful or handsome? In what ways would your life be different?
4. What are some negative results of being beautiful? Do you know people who are beautiful but unhappy?

2. Picture Focus

With a partner, talk about the picture. What do you think is happening?

3. Story Preview

Read the preview of the story and, with a partner, try to guess the meaning of the words in **bold** print.

For most of her life Elena was lucky. She was very beautiful and was used to receiving **compliments** on her beauty. Not only was she beautiful, but things always worked out well for her. She went to college and then married a handsome, successful man and had two fine children.

Things changed for her when she and her husband got a **divorce.**

After her husband left her, Elena felt bad about his **rejection** of her. One day, Elena bought an old mirror in an antique shop, and it changed her life. When she looked into the mirror, she felt younger and happier, and her **wrinkles** seemed to go away. The more she looked into the mirror, the younger she felt.

4. Using the Vocabulary

Fill in the blanks below with the **bold** words from the Story Preview above. Then, with a partner, compare your answers.

Many people feel that physical appearance is very important. Of course, people generally like to receive ____compliments____ on how young and attractive they look. Both men and women feel a sense of _____ when others don't want to associate with them because of their appearance or other physical qualities in general. For this reason, some people even begin to worry the first time they see _____ on their faces. Problems of physical appearance can even lead to the separation and _____ of some married couples.

5. Making Predictions

Read the first three paragraphs of the story. From these paragraphs and the Story Preview, try to predict what changes are likely to happen in Elena's life. Which of the following predictions is the most *probable?* Circle one or more of the choices or give an answer that you think is better.

1. Elena's children are angry about the divorce and refuse to see her again.

2. Her children sympathize with her and become closer to her.

3. The mirror makes her become beautiful again.

4. She meets a new man, marries him, and is happy again.

5. _____

Journal Writing In your journal, record your ideas about the life changes that Elena is likely to experience. After you read the story, reread what you wrote.

IDIOMS AND EXPRESSIONS	
pretty as a picture very pretty	**need space** want to live alone
happily ever after without any problems for your entire life	**take a drive** go out in a car
	feel blue feel depressed
went sour turned bad	**spotted** saw
cast a spell use magic (*on something or someone*)	**her eyes were drawn** she saw

6. Literary Term: Symbolism

A **symbol** is a thing (most often a concrete object of some type) that represents an idea or a group of ideas. For example, some common symbols in the mass media are a dove (as a sign of peace), a lion (as a symbol of courage), or a flag (as an emblem of a country).

Focus As you read "The Mirror," pay attention to the use of the magic mirror and any other mirrors that are mentioned. Try to think of the ideas that a mirror might represent.

About the Author

Judith Kay (1950–) was born in New York City and lived there until she got married. She has been a teacher, a textbook author, and a short-story writer. She received her M.A. in TESOL at Hunter College in New York and has been teaching most of her adult life. After teaching English as a Second Language at Marymount Manhattan College for a number of years, she moved to Florida, where she is currently teaching at Broward Community College.

The Mirror

Elena had always been called a beauty. When she was a little girl, people often stopped her mother to say, "What a beautiful little girl!" Often, strangers would bend over and say to Elena, "You're as pretty as a picture!" Elena had learned to smile and accept their compliments. Elena's mother had taught her to respond with a prompt "Thank you very much." By the time she was five, her beauty had become a natural part of her life, along with her toys, her pretty dresses, and her shiny, black patent leather shoes.

That was a long time ago. Fifty years had passed, and time had brought many changes to Elena's life. Now 55 years old, Elena was still pretty, but she had the face of a woman who, as people said, "*must* have been *beautiful* when she was younger."

In high school Elena had always been popular. She won the Prom Queen contest in her senior year, and she was so excited to wear the crown at the senior prom. Naturally, she loved being the center of attention. The prom had been a perfect evening, and she had hoped it would never end. She wanted to be happy forever – as happy as she was at that moment. Elena felt as though she were a beautiful princess in a fairy tale, one who could live happily ever after.

In college she met Jim, who became her husband. She married him right after their graduation. Jim was handsome and ambitious. He adored Elena and for years he would refer to her as "my bride." Their two children,

Margaret and Alan, were perfect as far as Elena was concerned. She used to say that they completed the picture of them as "the All-American family." Living in the lovely little suburban town of Greenville, Connecticut, they were happy, healthy, prosperous, and blessed with good luck.

And then one day it all went sour. What caused the change? Perhaps Elena had been *too* lucky. Or too pretty. She remembered the fairy tale of the witch who, out of jealousy toward a beautiful, young princess, cast a spell on her one day. Maybe someone secretly hated Elena and had wished her evil.

The way it happened was this. One day, after her two children had graduated from college and were living away from home, Jim came home from the office and said simply, "I'm not happy here anymore. I think I should move out. I need space."

Elena couldn't believe it. For once, she didn't know what to say. She just stood in front of Jim with her mouth open. All she could think was, "This is a bad dream. This can't be happening."

But Jim wanted out of the marriage, so Elena finally agreed to the divorce. She thought about it a great deal, and she realized she couldn't stay with someone who didn't love her anymore. His rejection of her was painful, but as time passed, she grew to accept it; and now the pain was more like a dull ache. That year had been a difficult one for Elena. She and Jim signed the final divorce papers in early January. It was now February 14 – Valentine's Day and Elena's birthday.

Valentine's Day had fallen on a depressing, cold, gray morning. But Alan, who was now living in Paris, called to wish her a Happy Birthday. He even sang it to her over the phone in the same off-key voice he had as a child. Margaret called and sent a beautiful bouquet of yellow roses. Elena cried when she opened the box and saw them nestled in the green tissue paper. Yes, it was sweet of her children to remember her birthday. She knew she should be grateful to have them, but she felt alone. She felt hollow, empty inside.

She realized she needed to get out of the house. She was feeling sorry for herself, and, of course, that was no good. She decided to plan a day in the country – a special day, since it was her birthday. She was going to force herself to have fun so she could push away the sadness.

It seemed to be working already. The

> *One day, after her two children had graduated from college and were living away from home, Jim came home from the office and said simply, "I'm not happy here anymore."*

thought of taking a drive cheered her up almost instantly. Obviously, it was staying around the house for too long that was making her feel blue. She dressed in warm clothes: a sweater, a fleece jacket, a wool scarf, and leather gloves. The car already had a full tank of gas. She would drive through the Berkshires and stop whenever and wherever she wanted. Maybe she'd even stay overnight at one of those quaint country inns. The feeling of freedom was exhilarating, and she was surprised to see herself smile as she looked in the car mirror. It was a long time since she remembered smiling.

Just outside of Lenox, Massachusetts, Elena spotted an antique shop. It was called Fanny Dolittle's. She had been there with Jim many years earlier. As she walked into the shop, the ringing of the little bell on the door announced her entrance. The owner of the shop, a balding, older man who looked as if he had just woken up from a nap, came out of the back room. He smoothed his hair as he smiled and apologized for not expecting anyone so late in the afternoon. Elena glanced at her watch for the first time since she had left home. It was four-thirty and beginning to get dark.

"I'm sorry. I didn't realize it was so late. I just wanted to look around. I haven't been here in years, and I remembered you had nice things," Elena said.

"Oh, that's all right. Take your time. If you need any help, just holler," the old man replied.

Elena examined some cut glass vases and a delicate china tea set. Then she wandered into another room, and her eyes were drawn to an antique hand mirror. She was surprised she even noticed it. Covered with lace, it lay on top of an old oak dresser. Elena picked up the mirror and stared at her reflection. "I look happy and younger," she murmured to herself.

The owner came over to Elena and asked whether she was looking for anything special.

"Yes. I was looking for a mirror," she replied. "How much is this one? There's no price on it."

He took a look at it. "That's strange," he said. "I never saw that piece before. My wife must have brought it in recently. If you want, I can call her at home and ask her."

"Would you, please?" Elena tried to control her excitement. She felt she absolutely had to have the mirror.

The owner went over to the phone near the cash register at the front of the store and called his wife. Elena looked at herself in the mirror again. She noticed that her eyes looked brighter and the small wrinkles around them seemed fainter. She smiled and thought, "What a wonderful mirror! It makes me feel younger. It makes me feel happy."

She walked to the front of the shop just as the owner had hung up the phone. "Well," he said, "my wife doesn't remember the mirror either, but when I described it to her, she thought we should sell it for about $50."

"That's fine. I'll take it," Elena said. "May I write you a check?"

"No problem. Shall I wrap it for you?"

"Yes," said Elena. "It's a birthday gift."

When she arrived home, Elena placed the mirror on the dresser in her bedroom. She unwrapped the paper and looked closely at the mirror. She marveled at the details on the oval silver frame and the delicate roses and leaves decorating the handle, with its single red garnet embedded in a rose at the base, just below the mirror. It was truly beautiful.

That night Elena slept better than she had in months. She went for a walk after breakfast and felt energetic. She almost forgot about the mirror until that evening when she was getting ready for bed. She picked it up, looked at herself, and smiled. "Every time I look at myself, I feel younger. Tonight I can't see any gray hairs. It's as if some magic in the mirror makes me younger," she said to herself. "But of course that isn't possible. I'm *imagining* I look younger." She put the mirror down. "I'm being silly and ridiculous."

Elena put the mirror in the top drawer of her dresser under some scarves. For a few days she didn't look at the mirror at all. She continued feeling energetic and happy.

She decided to go into town and have her hair done. When she arrived at Chez Charles, the hair salon she had been going to for over ten years,

> ■ ■ ■
>
> *"Tonight I can't see any gray hairs. It's as if some magic in the mirror makes me younger," she said to herself.*
>
> ■ ■ ■

everyone remarked how wonderful she looked. Charles, the owner, said, "Elena, you look so different! You look younger. What's your secret? Did you have some 'work' done? Whoever did it is marvelous!"

Elena thanked him for the compliment. She couldn't possibly tell him about the mirror. From the expression on his face, it was obvious he thought she had had plastic surgery. Fine – let him think that was the secret of her newfound youth.

She left the salon and went to the market for some ice cream, hot fudge, milk, Cheerios, and peanut butter. She seldom bought these things, but for some reason, she felt like having them. "I guess I'm indulging myself. Well, why not? I've been unhappy for so long. It's about time I started doing things that are fun."

When she got home later that afternoon, she took the mirror out again. Looking in the mirror had become a daily ritual. This time she was positive she saw a difference in her face. She looked as though she were in her early twenties again. Her skin had the glow of a young woman's. All her wrinkles were gone. The worry lines on her forehead were no longer there. It was eerie but wonderful.

That night when Elena made

dinner, she treated herself to a peanut butter and jelly sandwich with a glass of chocolate milk. For dessert she had a big dish of ice cream with hot fudge sauce. She ate her meal on the couch and watched television. Elena hardly ever watched TV before, but lately she seemed to enjoy it more and more. She usually loved to spend her time reading, but over the last few days she had had trouble concentrating. Also, she had come across a number of words that were unfamiliar to her, and she didn't want to bother looking them up in the dictionary.

The next morning, Elena had trouble waking up. She was having an old recurring dream that hadn't bothered her for many years. The last time was probably when she was very young. In her dream she was walking through a meadow and picking wildflowers. Suddenly, an ugly witch with long, straggly hair and red eyes chased her into a forest. The witch kept saying, "I'm going to get you and eat you." It was dark and cold in the forest, and the witch was getting closer and closer. Elena tried to scream, but the words wouldn't come out of her mouth. Finally, her mother and father came to save her.

She had often had this dream as a child, and it had always scared her. This morning when she woke up, her heart was beating rapidly, and her throat was dry. She felt like a scared child again.

A bit dizzy from her dream, Elena got out of bed and went over to the dresser. But something was wrong. Somehow, the dresser seemed too high for her to reach. Instead of looking down at the top of the dresser, she found herself standing on her toes to reach the mirror that lay on the dresser.

As she pulled the mirror handle to look at her reflection, she began to think that she had changed. She screamed and almost dropped the mirror. What she saw was a face that was very familiar to her. It was a face that was beautiful and young – *very* young. Staring back at her from the mirror were the big eyes and small face of a child.

1. *Understanding the Story*

With a partner, answer these questions.

1. What does Elena remember about herself when she was five years old?
2. How does Elena feel on the night of her senior prom?
3. What happens to Elena's marriage?
4. Who remembers Elena's birthday? What do they do?
5. How does Elena celebrate her birthday? What gift does she buy for herself?
6. What is strange about the mirror?
7. At what point do you first suspect something is wrong with the magic in the mirror?

2. *Vocabulary Comprehension*

Choose the word from the following list that best completes each of the sentences below. Do not use the same word more than once.

ridiculous	compliments	indulge	quaint
rejection	grateful	balding	reflection

1. It embarrassed Elena to get _____compliments_____ about her beauty, but she learned to say thank you.

2. When Jim wanted to divorce Elena, she cried because of his _____ of her.

3. Elena stopped at an old country inn that was _____ and charming.

4. Many men who are _____ use special treatments to stop the loss of their hair.

5. Elena knew other people would think she was _____ if she told them about the magic mirror.

6. Sometimes, when people are unhappy, they feel better after they _____ themselves with gifts or special foods.

7. The parents of the lost child were extremely happy and _____ to

the police officers who found him and brought him home.

8. When Elena looked at her _____ in the mirror, she saw herself as

younger and happier.

3. *Word Forms*

Complete the chart by filling in the various forms of the following words taken from "The Mirror." An X indicates that no form is possible. Use your dictionary if you need help. **Note:** There may be more than one possible word for the same part of speech.

VERB	NOUN	ADJECTIVE	ADVERB
_____	beauty	*beautiful*	_____
graduate	_____	_____	X
_____	_____	prosperous	_____
X	_____	jealous	_____
_____	marriage	_____	X
_____	_____	final	_____
X	_____	grateful	_____
_____	_____	ridiculous	_____
_____	expression	_____	_____
_____	_____	recurrent	_____
scare	_____	_____	X
_____	_____	familiar	_____

Work with a partner. Create sentences by using any word forms from the following combinations of words from the chart above:

1. beauty, marriage, prosperous   3. final, familiar, expression
2. scare, grateful, jealous   4. ridiculous, recurrent, graduate

4. Grammar: Count and Noncount Nouns

All nouns are either count nouns or noncount nouns.

A count noun is something that can be counted. It can be singular or plural.

Examples:
She dressed in warm clothes: **a sweater, a fleece jacket, a wool scarf,**
and **leather gloves.**
She took **two sweaters, two jackets, two scarves,** and **four gloves.**
In her dream she was walking through **a meadow** and picking
wildflowers.
Suddenly, **an ugly witch** . . . chased her into **a forest.**

Noncount nouns are nouns that are not counted. They represent things that are thought of as not being possible to separate (such as *bread, milk, water*).

Most noncount nouns are written in the singular form, and all are used with singular verbs.

Examples:
The car already had a full tank of **gas.**
She . . . went to the market for some **ice cream, hot fudge, milk,** . . .
and **peanut butter.**

5. Application

Read the sentences from the story. On the line next to each sentence, write the plural form of the **bold** word if it is a count noun. If the **bold** word is a noncount noun, write only *noncount* on the line.

1. When she was a little **girl,** people often stopped her mother to say, "What a

   beautiful little **girl**!" _____girls_____

2. They were happy, healthy, prosperous, and blessed with good **luck.**

   _____

3. Just outside of Lenox, Massachusetts, Elena spotted an antique **shop.**

   _____

4. The prom had been a perfect **evening**. . . . _____

5. The **owner** came over to Elena. . . . _____

6. Elena glanced at her **watch** for the first time since she had left home.

   _____

7. "I was looking for a **mirror.**" _____

8. She decided to go into town and have her **hair** done. _____

9. Margaret called and sent a beautiful **bouquet** of yellow roses.

   _____

10. It was obvious he thought she had had plastic **surgery.** _____

11. Elena put the mirror in the top **drawer** of her dresser. . . . _____

12. She was having an old recurring **dream** that hadn't bothered her for many

    years. _____

13. For dessert she had a big dish of **ice cream.** . . . _____

14. She ate her meal on the **couch** and watched television. _____

Editing Practice Remember that noncount nouns are always used with singular verbs. Edit the following paragraph by making sure that each noncount noun subject is modified by a verb in the singular form. First, underline all the noncount nouns. Then find the verb that modifies each noncount noun and change it from plural to singular if necessary.

It isn't easy to find a good marriage partner. You want to be married to someone you can trust. Honesty are a particularly important quality in a husband or wife. But happiness don't only depend on agreeing about the important things. Agreeing about little things is very important when you spend most of your time with someone. For example, food become important when you eat together every day. Do you and your partner like the same food? Cleaning the house is also important. Will you share this task? Responsibility for household chores are something you must agree on. Money can be a source of disagreement, too. Do you want to spend all your money or save some? Success in marriage depend on the small things as well as the large ones.

1. *Sharing Ideas*

Discuss the following questions with a partner or in a group:

1. For Elena, what are the advantages and disadvantages of being beautiful?
2. Why does Elena like the mirror so much? What does it do for her?
3. Why doesn't Elena tell Charles, her hairdresser, about the mirror?
4. Would you want to have a mirror like Elena's?

2. *Reading Between the Lines*

Practice reading between the lines. Answer the following questions:

1. How do you know Elena likes being beautiful?

_____

_____

2. When did Elena's life start to "go sour"?

_____

_____

3. What seems strange about the mirror before Elena buys it?

_____

_____

4. What would be Charles's reaction if Elena told him about the mirror?

_____

_____

5. What is the meaning of the dream Elena has? Why does she dream it again as an adult?

_____

_____

3. Analyzing the Story

Look back at the Literary Term on page 102. Make a diagram like the one below. In each box of your diagram, write one idea of what you think the mirror symbolizes. Then, under each idea, write in an example from the story that supports it. A sample answer is provided for you.

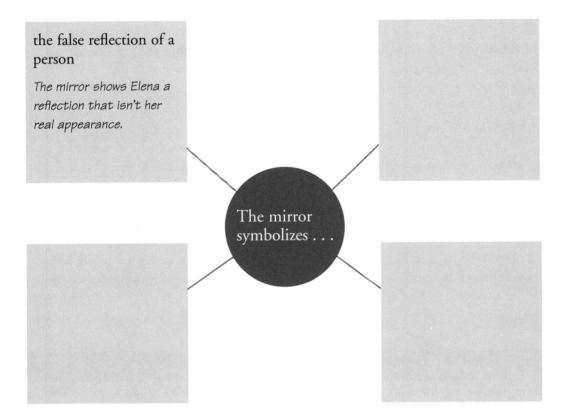

the false reflection of a person

The mirror shows Elena a reflection that isn't her real appearance.

The mirror symbolizes . . .

Pair Discussion   With a partner, compare what you have written in your charts. Correct any mistakes you find. Then discuss each other's ideas about the symbolism of the mirror. Do you agree or disagree?

4. Writing

Choose one of the following writing assignments:

1. Write a summary of the story in two to three paragraphs.
2. Do you feel the main character is being rewarded or punished in the story? Write a short composition to explain your point of view.
3. Describe what the advertising and entertainment industries could do to place a greater value on older people.

Summing Up

TAKE A CLOSER LOOK

1. Theme Comparison: Escape from Reality

In these stories, Margie and Elena both want to escape from the "reality" of daily life. It's a very appealing idea, but would we really like this if we could do it?

1. Do you think Margie would be happier if she could live in the days of her grandfather's grandfather? Do you think Elena is happier as a child?
2. Traveling – even if it's not through time – can be a way to escape reality. Reading and listening to music might also be considered as ways to escape. What are some other ways that people escape from "reality"?

2. Freewriting

Write the word *escape* on the top of a sheet of paper. Now write any words that come into your mind when you think of this word. For fifteen minutes, write about your ways of escaping from reality.

B **REVIEW**

1. Idioms and Expressions Review

The following story will use some of the idioms you learned in Part Three. Work with a partner or in a small group. Fill in the blanks with the correct idioms and expressions. The first letter of each answer is supplied.

pretty as a picture	went sour	feeling blue	cast a spell
happily ever after	spotted	betcha	eyes were drawn

Once upon a time, there was a princess who was as p_retty___ __as___

___a___ __picture__, but she was also lazy. Although there were many books in her castle library, she never read them. One day an evil witch, who was angry because her life w_____ _____ , saw the beautiful princess and

c_____ _____ _____ on her. The princess could not speak anymore.

The princess was sorry for herself and was f_____ _____. One day, her

e_____ _____ _____ to a book. She s_____ it on a table and

began reading it. Suddenly, she heard a voice. She turned and saw a little mouse

that could speak English. The mouse told her that he loved to read books, too.

He said he had read every book in the castle library. She wanted to speak to the

mouse, but of course she couldn't because of the witch's spell. Then the mouse

said, "I b_____ we can break the spell if we try really hard." The princess

kissed the mouse for being such a caring friend, and suddenly, he turned into a

handsome prince and she could speak again. They got married and lived

h_____ _____ _____.

2. Form Review

Underline all the nouns you can find in the following paragraph and label them **C** for count or **N** for noncount. The first sentence has been done for you.

>   C   N
>
> Elena's <u>problem</u> was her <u>beauty</u>. Because she was becoming less beautiful as
>
> she grew older, she suffered fear and loneliness. Her husband left her, and
>
> she had few friends. When she found the mirror in the country shop, her
>
> trouble really began. The mirror was magic that turned her into a child
>
> again. The lesson the story teaches is that character and personality are more
>
> important than outward appearance.

Write a short paragraph using at least three count nouns and three noncount nouns. Mark **C** or **N** above each noun in your paragraph.

PART FOUR

Turning Points

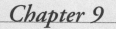

EVERY DAY, things happen to us, and we have to make decisions. We decide what to wear, where to shop, and what to do after class or work. But certain events force us to make important decisions and may even alter the course of our lives. The stories that follow are about people who are or have recently been faced with such turning points.

■ As you read, put yourself in the place of the main character. What is the turning point? Would you have acted differently? If so, what would you have done?

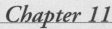

Chapter 11

HOME
– Gwendolyn Brooks

Chapter 9

You Go Your Way, I'll Go Mine William Saroyan

A PRE-READING

1. *Think Before You Read*

Answer the following questions:

1. What are some jobs that might sometimes involve giving people bad news about those they love?
2. What are some ways you might feel if you had a job like that and had to give someone very bad news?
3. What are some ways a person might react on receiving such news from a stranger? How would you feel if the person reacted in these ways?

2. Picture Focus

With a partner, talk about the picture. What do you think is happening?

3. Story Preview

Read the preview of the story and, with a partner, try to guess the meaning of the words in **bold** print.

Homer, a messenger, bicycles to Mrs. Sandoval's house with a telegram. He knows that the telegram says that her son has died in the war. As Homer waits for Mrs. Sandoval to open the door, he feels **eager** to meet this woman whose life will now be changed by death. But he's not just looking forward to meeting her. He is also feeling **awkward** – as though he doesn't know what to say or even how to stand – and almost as though the death is his **fault,** even though he knows he's just the messenger. He has no idea yet of how Mrs. Sandoval will react. And he has no idea of how her reaction will lead him to strangely mixed feelings of strong dislike and strong sympathy, or of how this **disgust** and **compassion** will change his life.

4. Using the Vocabulary

Fill in the blanks below with the **bold** words from the Story Preview above. Then, with a partner, compare your answers.

When friends suffer from the death of someone close to them, we feel great

_____compassion_____ for them. We want them to feel better; we are

_____ to see them smile again and move on with their lives.

However, sometimes our attempts to express our feelings seem _____.

When we can't quite say what we want to say, we may feel anger or even

_____ at our inability to say the right thing. If the person continues

to be sad, we may feel it's somehow our _____ for not helping

enough. We forget that people need time to recover from the death of a loved one.

5. Making Predictions

From the Story Preview, try to predict how Mrs. Sandoval will react when she hears the news of her son's death. Which of the following predictions do you think is the most *probable?* Circle one or more of the choices.

1. She'll yell at Homer and throw things at him.
2. She'll call the telegraph office to complain.
3. She'll pretend she hasn't heard and will offer Homer candy.
4. She'll cry.
5. She'll take Homer in her arms and call him her son.
6. She'll ask Homer to leave immediately.

Journal Writing   In your journal, explain why you chose your prediction(s).

IDIOMS AND EXPRESSIONS	
sit down with feel familiar or comfortable with **come right out and say** say directly **take the place of** substitute for, be there instead of	**in his heart** emotionally **at the same time** but also, however **just as good as** equal to, the same as

6. Literary Term: The Parts of a Plot

The **plot,** or story, of a piece of fiction often has four parts:

1. the **introduction,** where the main character(s) and the situation are introduced
2. the **complications,** or events, that happen once the situation has been introduced
3. the **climax** of the story, or the most important event, which usually occurs near the end and brings some change
4. the **conclusion** of the story, where the situation is resolved in some way and the story comes to an end

Focus   When you read "You Go Your Way, I'll Go Mine," think about how this story has these four parts of a plot.

About the Author

William Saroyan (1908–1981) grew up in Fresno, California, as part of an Armenian family that had migrated to the United States. He began writing as a teenager and soon sold his first short story to a Boston newspaper. Saroyan went on to write many other short stories as well as novels and plays. He based many of his characters on the memorable relatives and friends from his childhood. In 1940 Saroyan won the Pulitzer Prize for his play *The Time of Your Life*, now considered an American classic.

The story you are about to read is from the novel *The Human Comedy*. We see the world through the eyes of the main character, Homer, who learns about life and how to survive its challenges.

■ ■ ■ ■ ■ ■ ■ ■ ■ ■ ■ ■

You Go Your Way, I'll Go Mine

The messenger got off his bicycle in front of the house of Mrs. Rosa Sandoval. He went to
5 the door and knocked gently. He knew almost immediately that someone was inside the house. He could not hear anything, but he was sure the knock was bringing someone
10 to the door and he was most eager to see who this person would be – this woman named Rosa Sandoval who was now to hear of murder in the world and to feel it in herself. The door was
15 not a long time opening, but there was no hurry in the way it moved on its hinges. The movement of the door was as if, whoever she was, she had nothing in the world to fear. Then the door was open, and there she was. 20

To Homer the Mexican woman was beautiful. He could see that she had been patient all her life, so that now, after years of it, her lips were set in a gentle and saintly smile. But like all 25 people who never receive telegrams the appearance of a messenger at the front door is full of terrible implications. Homer knew that Mrs. Rosa Sandoval was shocked to see him. Her first word 30 was the first word of all surprise. She said "Oh," as if instead of a messenger she had thought of opening the door to someone she had known a long time and would be pleased to sit down with. Before she spoke again she studied Homer's eyes and Homer knew that she knew the message was not a welcome one.

"You have a telegram?" she said.

It wasn't Homer's fault. His work was to deliver telegrams. Even so, it seemed to him that he was part of the whole mistake. He felt awkward and almost as if he *alone* were responsible for what had happened. At the same time he wanted to come right out and say, "I'm only a messenger, Mrs. Sandoval. I'm very sorry I must bring you a telegram like this, but it is only because it is my work to do so."

"Who is it for?" the Mexican woman said.

"Mrs. Rosa Sandoval, 1129 G Street," Homer said. He extended the telegram to the Mexican woman, but she would not touch it.

"Are you Mrs. Sandoval?" Homer said.

"Please," the woman said. "Please come in. I cannot read English. I am Mexican. I read only *La Prensa* which comes from Mexico City." She paused a moment and looked at the boy standing awkwardly as near the door as he could be and still be inside the house.

"Please," she said, "what does the telegram say?"

"Mrs. Sandoval," the messenger said, "the telegram says –"

But now the woman interrupted him. "But you must *open* the telegram and *read* it to me," she said. "You have not opened it."

"Yes, ma'am," Homer said, as if he were speaking to a school teacher who had just corrected him.

He opened the telegram with nervous fingers. The Mexican woman stooped to pick up the torn envelope, and tried to smooth it out. As she did so she said, "Who sent the telegram – my son Juan Domingo?"

"No, ma'am," Homer said. "The telegram is from the War Department."

"War Department?" the Mexican woman said.

"Mrs. Sandoval," Homer said swiftly, "your son is dead. Maybe it's a mistake. Everybody makes a mistake, Mrs. Sandoval. Maybe it wasn't your son. Maybe it was somebody else. The telegram says it was Juan Domingo. But maybe the telegram is wrong."

The Mexican woman pretended not to hear.

"Oh, do not be afraid," she said. "Come inside. Come inside. I will bring you candy." She took the boy's arm and brought him to the table at the center of the room and there she made him sit.

"All boys like candy," she said. "I will bring you candy." She went into another room and soon returned with an old chocolate candy box. She opened the box at the table and in it Homer saw a strange kind of candy.

"Here," she said. "Eat this candy. All boys like candy."

Homer took a piece of the candy from the box, put it into his mouth, and tried to chew.

"You would not bring me a bad

telegram," she said. "You are a good boy – like my little Juanito when he was a little boy. Eat another piece." And she made the messenger take another piece of the candy.

Homer sat chewing the dry candy while the Mexican woman talked. "It is our own candy," she said, "from cactus. I make it for my Juanito when he come home, but *you* eat it. You are my boy too."

Now suddenly she began to sob, holding herself in as if weeping were a disgrace. Homer wanted to get up and run but he knew he would stay. He even thought he might stay the rest of his life. He just didn't know what else to do to try to make the woman less unhappy, and if she had *asked* him to take the place of her son, he would not have been able to refuse, because he would not have known how. He got to his feet as if by standing he meant to begin correcting what could not be corrected and then he knew the foolishness of this intention and became more awkward than ever. In his heart he was saying over and over again, "What can I do? What the hell can I do? I'm only the messenger."

The woman suddenly took him in her arms saying, "My little boy, my little boy!"

He didn't know why, because he only felt wounded by the whole thing, but for some reason he was sickened through all his blood and thought he would need to vomit. He didn't *dislike* the woman or anybody else, but what was happening to her seemed so wrong and so full of ugliness that he was sick and didn't know if he ever wanted to go on living again.

"Come now," the woman said. "Sit down here." She forced him into another chair and stood over him. "Let me look at you," she said. She looked at him strangely and, sick everywhere within himself, the messenger could not move. He felt neither love nor hate but something very close to disgust, but at the same time he felt great compassion, not for the poor woman alone, but for all things and the ridiculous way of their enduring and dying. He saw her back in time, a beautiful young woman sitting beside the crib of her infant son. He saw her looking down at this amazing human thing, speechless and helpless and full of the world to come. He saw her rocking the crib and he heard her singing to the child. Now look at her, he said to himself.

He was on his bicycle suddenly, riding swiftly down the dark street, tears coming out of his eyes and his mouth whispering young and crazy curses. When he got back to the telegraph office the tears had stopped, but everything else had started and he knew there would be no stopping them. "Otherwise I'm just as good as dead myself," he said, as if someone were listening whose hearing was not perfect.

1. *Understanding the Story*

With a partner, answer these questions.

1. Why is Homer going to Mrs. Sandoval's house? What are his feelings?
2. What is Homer's first impression of Mrs. Sandoval?
3. Why does Homer read the telegram to Mrs. Sandoval?
4. What is Mrs. Sandoval's first reaction to the telegram?
5. How does Homer act when Mrs. Sandoval offers him candy?
6. How does he feel when she begins to cry? How does he feel when she takes him in her arms and makes him sit down?
7. What does Homer finally do?
8. How does he feel when he gets back to the telegraph office?

2. *Vocabulary Comprehension*

Match each vocabulary word in the left column with the correct definition on the right. Write the letter of the definition in the space provided.

___e___	1. eager	a. silly, deserving to be laughed at
_____	2. wounded	b. very surprised, usually about something unpleasant
_____	3. compassion	
_____	4. implications	c. lasting, surviving
_____	5. shocked	d. sympathy
_____	6. welcome	e. looking forward to, showing great interest in
_____	7. enduring	f. say no
_____	8. awkwardly	g. suggested meanings
_____	9. ridiculous	h. very fast
_____	10. swiftly	i. hurt
_____	11. sob	j. cry
_____	12. refuse	k. wanted, desirable
		l. clumsily

3. Word Forms

Complete the chart by filling in the various forms of the following words taken from "You Go Your Way, I'll Go Mine." An X indicates that no form is possible. Use your dictionary if you need help. **Note:** There may be more than one possible word for the same part of speech.

VERB	NOUN	ADJECTIVE	ADVERB
X	_____	eager	*eagerly*
_____	murder	_____	_____
X	_____	gentle	_____
shock	_____	_____	_____
_____	surprise	_____	_____
X	_____	nervous	_____
X	_____	strange	_____
X	compassion	_____	_____

With a partner write a dialogue about a murder. One of you is the detective, and the other is a friend of the victim. Use at least eight word forms from the chart.

4. Grammar: Adverbs Versus Adjectives

An adverb modifies a verb, an adjective, another adverb, or a sentence.

Examples:
He went to the door and <u>knocked</u> gently. (modifies verb)
"I'm very <u>sorry</u> I must bring you a telegram like this. . . ." (modifies adjective)
He knew **almost** <u>immediately</u> that someone was inside the house. (modifies adverb)
<u>He was on his bicycle</u> suddenly. . . . (modifies sentence)

Many adverbs answer the question *How?* Others answer questions like *When?* (such as *now, then, soon, still, yet*), *How often?* (such as *often, seldom, never*), or *How much?* (such as *very, too, enough*).

Examples:
He was . . . riding **swiftly** down the dark street. . . . (How was he riding?)
She . . . **soon** returned with an old chocolate candy box. (When did she return?)
"I'm **very** sorry I must bring you a telegram like this. . . ." (How sorry does he feel?)

Many adverbs are formed by adding *-ly* to adjectives. However, many adverbs don't end in *-ly*, and some adjectives (such as *friendly*) end in *-ly*. To know whether a word is an adverb or adjective, look at the word it modifies. Remember, an adjective modifies a noun; an adverb modifies a verb, adjective, or adverb. Be careful! With a linking verb (such as *be, seem*), the word that follows the verb modifies the subject noun and is an adjective rather than an adverb.

Examples:
He <u>knew</u> almost **immediately** that someone was inside the house. (adverb – modifies verb)
Her lips were set in a gentle and **saintly** <u>smile</u>. (adjective – modifies noun)
<u>He</u> . . . became more **awkward** than ever. (adjective – with linking verb *become*, modifies noun)

5. Application

The following sentences are from the story. For each sentence, choose the correct word from the alternatives in parentheses and write it on the line. Draw an arrow from the word you choose to the word it modifies. Then, working with a partner, reread the story and find six adjectives that can be made into *-ly* adverbs. Write a sentence for each of the adverbs. The sentences can be about the story or anything else.

1. He went to the door and knocked _____*gently*_____. (gentle, gently)

2. Her lips were set in a _____ (gentle, gently) and saintly smile.

3. He felt _____ (awkward, awkwardly) and almost as if he *alone* were responsible for what had happened.

4. She . . . looked at the boy standing _____ (awkward, awkwardly) as near the door as he could be and still be inside the house.

5. She opened the box . . . and in it Homer saw a _____ (strange, strangely) kind of candy.

6. She looked at him _____ (strange, strangely) and . . . the messenger could not move.

Editing Practice Edit the following paragraph by making sure that all adjectives and adverbs are used correctly. If an adjective is used where the word should be an adverb, change the word to its adverbial form. If an adverb is used where the word should be an adjective, change it to its adjectival form.

Last Saturday, our school held its annual talent show. In the morning, there was an art exhibit and in the afternoon students who could sing, play a musical instrument, or dance nice performed in the auditorium. I got up late and had to move quick to get to the art exhibit before it ended. Although many of the pictures were lovely, my favorite was a picture of a beach that was beautiful painted by a senior. Among the performers, I particularly liked a ballet dancer who was so gracefully. I've always wanted to be a graceful dancer, but I'm not. I did get on stage, though. I sing with a group, and we performed a couple of songs. Our friends said we were greatly and sang terrifically – but we didn't win first prize.

D | THINKING ABOUT THE STORY

1. Sharing Ideas

Discuss the following questions with a partner or in a group:

1. Why does Mrs. Sandoval treat Homer the way she does?
2. How do Homer's feelings about what he can and should do for Mrs. Sandoval change during the story?
3. In the end, Homer feels that what he has learned makes it possible for him to truly live. What has Homer learned?
4. The phrase *go one's (own) way* usually means "to act as one chooses, independently of others." What does the title of the story mean? Several interpretations are possible. For example, it might mean that Homer realizes that he can't really help Mrs. Sandoval – that they must each go their own way. Or, it might mean that Homer chooses to have compassion even if this isn't the world's usual way. Or, the title might have one or more other meanings. What do you think? Why?

2. Reading Between the Lines

Practice reading between the lines. Circle the letter of the answer that best completes each of the following statements:

1. When Homer tried to give Mrs. Sandoval the telegram, she didn't want to take it because
   a. she didn't know how to read English.
   b. she was quite certain it would be bad news.
   c. she had never received a telegram before and didn't know what to do with it.

2. Mrs. Sandoval offers Homer candy because
   a. even though she is upset, she sees he feels awkward, and she wants to make him more comfortable.
   b. as the mother of a son, she knows that boys likes candy.
   c. she associates him with her son, whose death she wants to deny.

3. In the last paragraph, the line "everything else had started and he knew there would be no stopping them" refers to
   a. the pressures of everyday life.
   b. war and the deaths and sadness it causes.
   c. Homer's feelings for and about other people.

3. Analyzing the Story

Look back at the Literary Term on page 120. The following chart shows the parts of a story. The events in this story are listed below the chart. Show where the events go in the chart by writing the numbers in the appropriate places.

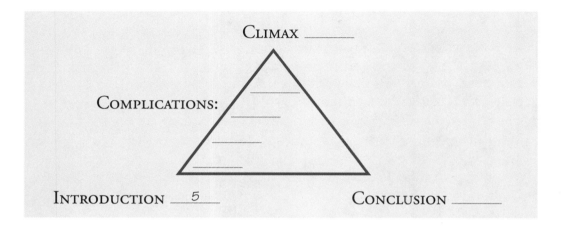

1. Mrs. Sandoval offers Homer candy.
2. Back at the telegraph office, Homer realizes that everything has changed for him.
3. Mrs. Sandoval takes Homer in her arms, and Homer feels that everything in the world is wrong.
4. Mrs. Sandoval begins to sob, and Homer wants to make her less unhappy.
5. Homer goes to Mrs. Sandoval's door, feeling eager to meet her.
6. Homer has a feeling of disgust but also great compassion toward all things and leaves Mrs. Sandoval's house crying.
7. Mrs. Sandoval asks Homer to read the telegram to her.

Pair Discussion   With a partner, compare your charts. Correct any mistakes you find. Then discuss the following question: In which parts of the story is an attitude toward war expressed? Find sentences to support your opinions.

4. Writing

Choose one of the following writing assignments:

1. Write a summary of the story in two to three paragraphs. Be sure to include all the major events. Look at the chart above if you need help.
2. Write a letter that Mrs. Sandoval sent to her son, Juan, before he was killed.
3. Look up the word *compassion* in your dictionary. Give examples of compassion from your own experience.

Chapter 10

Snake Dance COREY FORD

A PRE-READING

1. Think Before You Read

Answer the following questions:

1. How would you describe an ideal college experience?
2. Have you ever had to work at a job you were ashamed of? What did you tell other people about your job?
3. Have you ever had to give up something you wanted very much so that you could help another person?

2. Picture Focus

With a partner, talk about the picture. What do you think is happening?

3. Story Preview

Read the preview of the story and, with a partner, try to guess the meaning of the words in **bold** print.

> Jerry's parents are proud that he is in college. He is talking to his mother on the phone and telling her he has joined a **fraternity** and lives with the men in the fraternity house instead of a **dormitory.** He also tells her that he doesn't need money from home because he has won a **scholarship** for being such a good football player.
>
> While Jerry is in the phone booth, a parade of students in a **snake dance** to celebrate a football victory comes down the street. Jerry explains that he has scored two **touchdowns** in the game, and he holds out the phone so that his mother can hear the band and the students celebrating.

4. Using the Vocabulary

Fill in the blanks below with the **bold** words from the Story Preview above. Then, with a partner, compare your answers.

When a college football team wins, the fans celebrate in many ways. Sometimes, for example, students celebrate by doing a _____snake dance_____ – marching in a long line that moves from one side of the street to the other.

A good football player can often get a _____ to pay for college, which could be too expensive without one. A player who frequently scores points by making _____ is especially valuable.

Football players and athletes in general often like to join a _____ , where the male students live and have their own rooms. In this way, their situation is better than that of other students who live in a regular _____ , where students typically have to share a room.

5. Making Predictions

From the Story Preview, you know that Jerry tells his mother how well he is doing at college. But the beginning of the story shows that Jerry is nervous. Read the first two paragraphs (lines 1–26) and try to predict why he is nervous. Circle your choice or give an answer that you think is better.

Jerry is nervous because

1. he is going to fail in some of his classes.

2. he doesn't want to miss the snake dance.

3. he shouldn't be smoking since he needs to stay in shape to play football.

4. _____

Journal Writing   In your journal, explain why you chose your answer.

IDIOMS AND EXPRESSIONS	
holding it waiting for a short time while the person you're talking to on the telephone does something else	**chew the fat** talk
	hang up end a phone call
fished looked for	**the gang** a group of people who are friendly with each other
laid up sick in bed	**took 'em** won, beat them
on account of because of	**heck** a slang expression to add emphasis to a statement or question
the time of my life a great time	**soft job** easy job with a good salary
swell nice	**babe** young woman; woman
sitting pretty secure, rich	

6. Literary Term: Surprise Ending

A **surprise ending** is a sudden and unexpected ending. Many American short-story writers are noted for this technique.

Focus   When you read, look for the sentences that reveal the "surprise."

About the Author

Corey Ford (1902–1969) was a well-known humorist, essayist, and short-story writer, some of whose work appeared in magazines such as *Collier's*, *The New Yorker*, and *The Saturday Evening Post*.

During his career, Ford traveled extensively to remote parts of the world. When not traveling, Ford lived in New Hampshire, where he pursued his hobbies – hunting and fishing. Ford shared his home with his dog, Cinder, the inspiration for his book *Every Dog Should Have a Man*. His other books include *The Day Nothing Happened*, *How to Guess Your Age*, *Has Anyone Seen Me Lately?* and *What Every Bachelor Knows*. This last title is a defense of his choice to remain single, as he put it, "to make some unknown girl happy."

Ford's work also treats serious themes, as you will see when you read "Snake Dance."

Snake Dance

"Hello. That you, mom? . . . Oh, I'm sorry, operator, I thought I was connected with . . . No, I'm trying to get long-distance . . . What? Centerville, Ohio, twelve ring five, I told that other operator . . . What? . . . I *am* holding it."

5

He fished nervously in his pocket for a pack of cigarettes, pulled one cigarette out of the pack with his thumb and forefinger, and stuck it swiftly between his lips. He glanced at his watch and scowled. The game had been over for a half hour. The snake dance would be coming down the street this way any minute now. With his free hand he tore a match from the paper safe, and propped the telephone receiver for a moment between shoulder and ear while he struck the match on the flap. As he put the match to the tip of the cigarette, a thin voice

10

15

20

rasped vaguely inside the receiver, and he whipped out the match.[1]

"Hello. Mom? . . . Oh, I'm sorry," he mumbled. "How much?" He took a handful of silver from his pocket and began to drop the coins into the slot of the pay telephone. He could hear someone speaking above the echoing reverberations inside the phone.

"What? Oh, mom? Hello, mom. This is Jerry. I say, this is – Can you hear me now? . . . Sure, I can hear you fine. . . . Sure, I'm all right. I'm fine. And you? . . . That's fine.

"Mom" – and his voice seemed to falter for a fraction of a second. Then: "How is he? Is there any change?"

There was a tiny silence.

"Oh." His voice was a little duller when he spoke again. "I see. Yeh. This afternoon, eh? And that other specialist, he said the same thing? Um-hmm . . . Oh, sure, sure. No, of course, mom, there's nothing to worry about. No, I'm not worried; I only just called to find out if there was any change, that was all . . . Did they say if he could ever – I mean, can he move his arms any yet?" He gulped. "Well, that doesn't mean anything, really . . . No, of course, all those things take time. Sure, a year, or maybe even less . . . What?"

He took a second cigarette out of his pocket and thrust it between his lips nervously. He lit it from the stub of the first one and ground out the stub beneath his heel.

"What money? Oh, you mean I sent you last week? Now, mom," impatiently, "I told you all about that already in the letter, didn't I? . . . Sure it's a scholarship. I got it for playing football. And so naturally I didn't need all that money you and pop had been saving up for me to go to college, and so I just thought maybe, with pop being laid up now for a while and all . . .

"Where? Why, right here." He frowned. "No, this isn't exactly a dormitory; it's – I live here in the fraternity house, you see. Sure I'm in a fraternity. It's the one pop wanted me to join, too, tell him . . . No, honest, mom, it doesn't cost me a cent for my room. It's on account of my football."

He opened the folding door a little. He thought he could hear the band in the distance.

"Who, me? Homesick? Not so you'd notice it." He laughed. "I'm having the time of my life here. Everybody's so swell. I know practically everybody here at Dover already. They even all call me by my first name. Say, if you don't think I'm sitting pretty, you ought to see my fraternity house here." He gazed out through the glass door of the phone booth.

"Every night the fellows sit around

"I'm having the time of my life here. Everybody's so swell."

[1] *whipped out the match:* waved the match quickly until it went out.

and we drink beer and chew the fat till . . . Oh, no. No, mom. Just beer. Or usually we just go down to Semple's for a milk shake . . . No, that's only the drugstore . . . No." He smiled slowly. "I promised you I wouldn't drink, mom."

In the distance now he could hear the sound of the band approaching.

"Well, mom, I gotta hang up now. The gang'll be here in a minute. We're having a celebration after the game today. We played Alvord – took 'em sixteen to nothing. . . . Sure I did, the whole game; you oughta seen me in there. I made two touchdowns. Everybody's going down to Semple's after the game, and I gotta be ready, because of course they'll all want me to be there too. Can you hear the band now?"

It was growing louder, and the eager voices in the snake dance could be heard above the brasses, chanting the score of the game in time with the band.

"Now, listen, mom. One other little thing before they get here. Mom, see, I'm going to be sending you about ten or twelve dollars or so each week from now on until pop is better. . . . No, mom. Heck, I got plenty. Sure, they always fix you up with a soft job if you're a good enough player. The alumni do it. . . . Here they are now. Hear them?"

The band had halted outside. Someone led a cheer.

"That's for me, mom. . . . Sure. Didn't I practically win the game for them today? Hear that?" He kicked open the door of the phone booth.

He held the receiver toward the open door of the phone booth. They were calling, "Jerry!" "Hey, Jerry, hang up on that babe!"

"Hear that, mom? Now, good-bye. And look, by the way, if you should ever happen to see Helen," he added carelessly, "tell her I'm sorry I couldn't ask her up to the freshman dance like I'd planned, but with the football season and my scholarship and all – Tell her, mom. She – she didn't answer my last letter. OK, mom. Tell pop everything's OK, see? Now don't worry . . . 'Bye."

He replaced the receiver slowly on the hook and stared at the mouthpiece a moment. As he opened the door and stepped out of the booth, he could see his reflection for a moment in the tall mirror behind the soda fountain – the familiar white cap, the white jacket with "Semple's" stitched in red letters on the pocket. The crowd was lined along the soda fountain, shouting, "Jerry!" "Milk shake, Jerry!"

1. Understanding the Story

With a partner, answer these questions.

1. Why is Jerry calling his mother?
2. What does Jerry tell his mother is his source of money?
3. What is happening while Jerry is on the phone?
4. What does Jerry tell his mother that isn't true?
5. Where does Jerry work? What does he do?
6. Why does Jerry lie to his mother?

2. Vocabulary Comprehension

Match each vocabulary word in the left column with its **antonym** (a word or phrase with the opposite meaning) in the right column. Write the letter of the antonym in the space provided.

_e_	1. approach	a. keep going, continue
_____	2. scowl	b. earpiece
_____	3. glance	c. nearby
_____	4. halt	d. unknown
_____	5. nervous	e. move away
_____	6. vague	f. gaze
_____	7. dull	g. general doctor, family doctor
_____	8. specialist	h. speak clearly
_____	9. distant	i. calm
_____	10. mouthpiece	j. bright
_____	11. familiar	k. clear
_____	12. mumble	l. smile

Write sentences of your own using three words from the left column. Compare your sentences with a partner. Correct any mistakes you find.

3. Word Forms

Complete the chart by filling in the various forms of the following words taken from "Snake Dance." An X indicates that no form is possible. Use your dictionary if you need help. **Note:** There may be more than one possible word for the same part of speech.

Verb	Noun	Adjective	Adverb
X	_____	nervous	*nervously*
X	_____	eager	_____
_____	reflection	_____	_____
play	_____	_____	_____
_____	_____	celebratory, celebrated	X
_____	crowd	_____	X

Work with a partner. Write sentences using a verb, a noun, an adjective, and an adverb from the chart above.

4. Grammar: Regular and Irregular Verbs

Regular verbs form their past tense by adding -*d* or -*ed*. Examples:

Present	Past	Past Participle
start	started	started
work	worked	worked

Irregular verbs fall into a number of different categories. The verbs below are given as examples. Check the Appendix on page 208 for a list of irregular verbs.

Present	Past	Past Participle
burst	burst	burst
drink	drank	drunk
give	gave	given
send	sent	sent

5. *Application*

Complete each sentence below with the correct past tense form of the verb in parentheses.

1. I ____thought____ (think) you were a student in college on a football scholarship.

2. The professor _____ (read) the test papers until 2 A.M.

3. You were the person who _____ (help) me most at school.

4. Margaret is very excited because she _____ (win) the scholarship.

5. We were the first ones on our street who _____ (play) football in college.

6. John _____ (make) the touchdown just in time to help the team win the game.

7. He _____ (become) a good football player, and his team loved him.

8. He _____ (break) the record for the most touchdowns in a game.

9. The crowd _____ (cheer) when the favorite team won.

10. We all _____ (go) home in a good mood after our team's victory.

11. I _____ (invite) some friends for dinner at my house Saturday night.

12. My friends and I were having such a good that I _____ (forget) about a paper that was due Monday.

13. Sunday morning, I _____ (remember) the paper and _____ (begin) to work on it.

14. I _____ (finish) the paper Sunday night and _____ (feel) that I had done a good job.

1. *Sharing Ideas*

Discuss the following questions with a partner or in a group:

1. Are lies sometimes excusable? Why or why not?
2. Is there any way Jerry could have solved his problem other than quitting school?
3. Do you respect Jerry for his sacrifice? Why or why not?
4. At any point in the story, did you suspect that Jerry wasn't telling the truth? If so, which point was it?

2. *Reading Between the Lines*

Practice reading between the lines. Circle the letter of the best answer.

1. How do you know Jerry is worried about his father?
   a. He calls home and sends money to his parents.
   b. He tells his mother he is worried.
   c. He's planning to go home and visit his father.
   d. He tells his mother he's quitting school.

2. Which of the following quotations shows that Jerry is a good son?
   a. "We're having a celebration after the game today."
   b. "I made two touchdowns."
   c. "I'm having the time of my life here."
   d. "I promised you I wouldn't drink, mom."

3. Why didn't Helen answer Jerry's letter?
   a. She goes to another school too far away.
   b. She was insulted because Jerry didn't invite her to the dance.
   c. She doesn't like Jerry.
   d. She's too busy to write.

4. When Jerry's mother hears the students calling Jerry's name, she thinks
   a. they want Jerry to get off the phone.
   b. they want Jerry to join them.
   c. they like Jerry because he helped win the football game.
   d. they're angry with Jerry.

3. Analyzing the Story

Look back at the Literary Term on page 132. Make a chart like the one below. The author's way of making the surprise ending effective is to have Jerry say things in such a way that his mother misunderstands them. Fill out your chart to see how Ford does this. The first one is done for you.

Jerry Says That . . .	His Mother Thinks That . . .	The Truth Is That . . .
he got a football scholarship and doesn't need the money his parents had saved for him.	*the money Jerry sent her is from the scholarship.*	*the money Jerry sent his mother is part of his salary from Semple's.*
he's having a great time and everybody in the town knows him.		
his mother would like his fraternity house if she could see it.		
he made two touchdowns in the football game that afternoon, and everybody will expect him to go to Semple's to celebrate.		
he has plenty of money because the alumni always arrange for a good football player to get a "soft job."		
the students are cheering for him.		

Pair Discussion With a partner, compare what you have written in your charts. Correct any mistakes you find. Then discuss whether you think there are any other "misunderstandings" in the story.

4. Writing

Choose one of the following writing assignments:

1. Write a summary of the story in two to three paragraphs. Be sure to include all the major points. Look at the chart you made for Analyzing the Story if you need help.
2. Imagine you are Helen, Jerry's girlfriend from his hometown. Write a letter to Jerry.
3. Jerry decides to apply for a scholarship. Write a letter he could use to explain why he deserves to receive the scholarship.
4. Imagine you are Jerry's mother and you find out the truth. Write a letter to Jerry.
5. Imagine you are Jerry and it's ten years later. Write about what has happened in your life since the story ended.
6. Write about a time when you or someone you know lied in order to protect someone else. Do you think the lie was justified? Why or why not?

Chapter 11

Home GWENDOLYN BROOKS

A | PRE-READING

1. Think Before You Read

Answer the following questions:

1. What are some of the things you like about your home?
2. Have you ever wanted to move? Did you ever fear that you would have to move?
3. Have you ever moved to a new town, city, or country? How did you feel?
4. Do you like or dislike change?

2. Picture Focus

With a partner, talk about the picture. What do you think is happening?

3. Story Preview

Read the preview of the story and, with a partner, try to guess the meaning of the words in **bold** print.

Maud Martha's parents are **homeowners** who are worried that they may have to move out of their house. Everyone is waiting for Papa to come back home from a trip to the Home Owners' **Loan** Company, the company that lent them the money to buy their house. Maud Martha's father has gone there to ask for an **extension** on the loan so that they can pay it back over a longer period of time. The family does not have enough money to make the regular payments. If the company doesn't give Papa an extension on the loan, the family will lose their home.

4. Using the Vocabulary

Fill in the blanks below with the **bold** words from the Story Preview above. Then, with a partner, compare your answers.

In order to buy a home and become ____homeowners____ , many people have to borrow money from a bank or another type of company that lends money to buy apartments, houses, and other types of property. Any _____ that a bank provides has to be repaid according to a schedule set by the bank. When people cannot repay the money exactly according to the schedule, they sometimes are able to get the bank to give them more time or to change the schedule. This type of _____ on repayment can mean all the difference to some people whose incomes are not very high.

5. Making Predictions

From the Story Preview, think ahead to what will happen to the family. Which of the following predictions do you think is the most *probable?* Circle your choice or give an answer that you think is better.

1. Papa will get an extension on the loan.

2. Papa will get an extension on the loan, but he still won't be able to pay it.

3. The family will move to an apartment.

4. The bank will refuse to give him an extension on the loan.

5. _____

Journal Writing   In your journal, write your answer and explain why you chose it. Then look back at your answer after you read the story.

IDIOMS AND EXPRESSIONS

jardiniere a decorative pot for plants

slip part of a plant

extension extra time given by a bank or loan company to pay one's monthly mortgage

flat apartment

doing the firing starting a coal fire in the furnace to heat the house

mechanical birds artificial *(not real)* birds

sun parlor room like an enclosed porch

dragged on continued to live with difficulty

---

6. Literary Term: Realism

In literature, **realism** gives us a picture of life as it really is. Stories of realism deal with everyday problems that most people encounter. Sometimes, the characters overcome their problems; other times, they don't. In the story "Home," a family has to face the possibility of losing its home.

Focus   As you read, look for the problems in the story that are very much like the problems people typically have in everyday life. Try to imagine you are one of the characters. How would you feel? How would you deal with the prospect of having to move?

About the Author

Born in Topeka, Kansas, Gwendolyn Brooks (1917–2000) lived most of her life in Chicago. The first African-American author to win the Pulitzer Prize – in 1950, for her poetry collection, *Annie Allen* – she became famous for portraying the ordinary lives of people in the African-American community. In 1985, she became the first African-American woman to be elected to the National Institute of Arts and Letters.

As a young child, Brooks began reading and writing poetry. Her parents encouraged her interest in literature and took her to poetry readings by African-American authors. Throughout her adolescent years and early twenties, Brooks's poems appeared in various magazines. In 1945, she published a volume of poetry entitled *A Street in Bronzville*, which won her national recognition as one of America's leading poets. From 1989 until her death, she was Distinguished Professor of Literature at Chicago State University.

The story you are about to read, "Home," is a chapter from Brooks's novel *Maud Martha*.

Home

What had been wanted was this always, this always to last, the talking softly on this porch, with the snake plant in the jardiniere in the southwest corner, and the obstinate slip from Aunt Eppie's magnificent Michigan fern at the left side of the friendly door.

Mama, Maud Martha, and Helen rocked slowly in their rocking chairs, and looked at the late afternoon light on the lawn and at the emphatic iron of the fence and at the poplar tree. These things might soon be theirs no longer. Those shafts and pools of light, the tree, the graceful iron, might soon be viewed possessively by different eyes.

Papa was to have gone that noon, during his lunch hour, to the office of the Home Owners' Loan. If he had not succeeded in getting another extension, they would be leaving this house in which they had lived for more than fourteen years. There was little hope. The Home Owners' Loan was hard. They sat, making their plans.

"We'll be moving into a nice flat somewhere," said Mama. "Somewhere on South Park, or Michigan, or in Washington Park Court." Those flats, as the girls and Mama knew well, were burdens on wages twice the size of Papa's. This was not mentioned now.

"They're much prettier than this old house," said Helen. "I have friends I'd just as soon not bring here. And I have other friends that wouldn't come down this far for anything, unless they were in a taxi."

Yesterday, Maud Martha would have attacked her. Tomorrow she might. Today she said nothing. She merely gazed at a little hopping robin in the tree, her tree, and tried to keep the fronts of her eyes dry.

"Well, I do know," said Mama, turning her hands over and over, "that I've been getting tireder and tireder of doing that firing. From October to April, there's firing to be done."

"But lately we've been helping, Harry and I," said Maud Martha. "And sometimes in March and April and in October, and even in November, we could build a little fire in the fireplace. Sometimes the weather was just right for that."

She knew, from the way they looked at her, that this had been a mistake. They did not want to cry.

But she felt that the little line of white, sometimes ridged with smoked purple, and all that cream-shot saffron[1] would never drift across any western sky except that in back of this house. The rain would drum with as sweet a dullness nowhere but here. The birds on South Park were mechanical birds, no better than the poor caught canaries in those "rich" women's sun parlors.

> "It's just going to kill Papa!" burst out Maud Martha. He loves this house! He lives *for this house!*"

"It's just going to kill Papa!" burst out Maud Martha. "He loves this house! He *lives* for this house!"

"He lives for us," said Helen. "It's us he loves. He wouldn't want the house, except for us."

"And he'll have us," added Mama, "wherever."

"You know," Helen sighed, "if you want to know the truth, this is a relief. If this hadn't come up, we would have gone on, just dragged on, hanging out here forever."

[1] *saffron:* a yellow-orange color.

"It might," allowed Mama, "be an act of God. God may just have reached down and picked up the reins."

"Yes," Maud Martha cracked in, "that's what you always say – that God knows best."

Her mother looked at her quickly, decided the statement was not suspect, looked away.

Helen saw Papa coming. "There's Papa," said Helen.

They could not tell a thing from the way Papa was walking. It was that same dear little staccato walk, one shoulder down, then the other, then repeat, and repeat. They watched his progress. He passed the Kennedys', he passed the vacant lot, he passed Mrs. Blakemore's. They wanted to hurl themselves over the fence, into the street, and shake the truth out of his collar. He opened his gate – the gate – and still his stride and face told them nothing.

"Hello," he said.

Mama got up and followed him through the front door. The girls knew better than to go in too.

Presently Mama's head emerged. Her eyes were lamps turned on.

"It's all right," she exclaimed. "He got it. It's all over. Everything is all right."

The door slammed shut. Mama's footsteps hurried away.

"I think," said Helen, rocking rapidly, "I think I'll give a party. I haven't given a party since I was eleven. I'd like some of my friends to just casually see that we're homeowners."

> *They wanted to hurl themselves over the fence, into the street, and shake the truth out of his collar.*

1. *Understanding the Story*

With a partner, answer these questions.

1. Why is the family waiting impatiently for Papa to come home?
2. How long has the family been living in the house?
3. How do Mama's and Helen's reactions differ from Maud Martha's?
4. What is the surprise at the end of the story?
5. What does Helen plan to do?

2. *Vocabulary Comprehension*

Read each of the following sentences from the story. Then circle the letter of the answer that gives the correct meaning for each word in **bold** print.

1. The tree, the graceful iron, might soon be viewed **possessively** by different eyes.
   a. with feelings of anger
   b. with feelings of ownership
   c. with feelings of envy
   d. with feelings of pride

2. She merely gazed at a little **hopping** robin. . . .
   a. jumping
   b. limping
   c. flying
   d. running

3. They could not tell a thing from the way Papa was walking. It was that same dear little **staccato** walk. . . .
   a. with short, quick steps
   b. with long, nervous steps
   c. with smooth, easy steps
   d. with slow, happy steps

4. Papa's **stride** told them nothing.
   a. walk
   b. look
   c. face
   d. expression

5. Presently Mama's head **emerged**.
   a. changed expression
   b. moved back and forth
   c. came into view
   d. turned around

6. Those flats . . . **were burdens on wages**. . . .
   a. gave the renters extra money every month
   b. cost more than working people could easily afford
   c. helped the renters to lower their taxes
   d. were expensive but very nice places to live

7. They wanted to **hurl** themselves over the fence, into the street, and shake the truth out of his collar.
   a. put
   b. throw
   c. place
   d. take

8. The rain would **drum** with as sweet a dullness nowhere but here.
   a. start and stop
   b. make a light noise
   c. fall heavily
   d. make a steady, rhythmic sound

9. "You know," Helen sighed, "if you want to know the truth, this is a **relief**."
   a. end of something unpleasant
   b. beginning of a new experience
   c. difficult situation
   d. disappointment

3. Word Forms

Complete the chart by filling in the various forms of the following words taken from "Home." An X indicates that no form is possible. Use your dictionary if you need help. **Note:** There may be more than one possible word for the same part of speech.

VERB	NOUN	ADJECTIVE	ADVERB
X	_____	obstinate	_obstinately_
X	_____	magnificent	_____
_____	_____	emphatic	_____
_____	_____	_____	possessively
_____	_____	hopping	X
hurl	_____	_____	X
stride	_____	_____	
emerge	_____	_____	X
burden	_____	_____	X

With a partner, write a letter to a friend in which you use some of the word forms above. You might, for example, describe an obstinate person who has become a burden.

4. Grammar: Future with Would and Might

In fiction, events are usually talked about in the past tense. Since the context of the story is the past, the future is described differently. Instead of using *will* for the future, the author typically uses *would* or *might*. (Other constructions also exist, but we will concentrate on these two.)

Examples:
They **would** be leaving this house in which they had lived for more than fourteen years.
The tree, the graceful iron, **might** soon be viewed possessively by different eyes.

5. Application

Work with a partner. Find examples of sentences in the story in which *would* or *might* refer to the future. Copy those sentences into the first column of the chart below. Look for sentences with *would* or *might* plus verb form (not *would have* or *might have* plus verb form). In the second column, explain what situation they refer to. Examples from the grammar section are provided below as a model.

SENTENCE	FUTURE SITUATION
They **would** be leaving this house in which they had lived for more than fourteen years.	If Papa doesn't get an extension on the loan, the family will have to leave the house.
The tree, the graceful iron, **might** soon be viewed possessively by different eyes.	If Papa doesn't get an extension on the loan, someone else will own the tree.

1. *Sharing Ideas*

Discuss the following questions with a partner or in a group:

1. Why is Maud Martha so attached to her home?
2. What do you think happens to families who can't find the money to pay the interest on their mortgage? Does this situation occur in other countries?
3. How do the characters in the story feel about Papa? What kind of man is he?
4. Did you guess the end of the story correctly? If not, what did you think would happen?
5. Could the story have had an unhappy ending? If so, what would each character say when she heard the bad news?

2. *Reading Between the Lines*

Practice reading between the lines. Circle the letter of the answer that best completes each of the following statements:

1. We can assume that the story is not set in modern times because of the reference to
   a. a loan company.
   b. doing the firing.
   c. a snake plant.

2. Maud Martha doesn't attack Helen for criticizing their home (lines 40–54) because
   a. Maud Martha knows Helen will get mad if she attacks her.
   b. Maud Martha is afraid Papa won't get the extension and they will have to move.
   c. Maud Martha would really prefer to live in a nice apartment.

3. Only one of the women in the family is honest about facing up to life's problems. This person is
   a. Helen.
   b. Mama.
   c. Maud Martha.

3. Analyzing the Story

Look back at the Literary Term on page 144 and think about the real-life problems that the author describes in "Home." Make a chart like the one below. Complete your chart with as many real-life problems as you can find, and then give examples of how such problems come up in everyday life. An example has been provided for you.

PROBLEMS IN THE STORY	PROBLEMS IN EVERYDAY LIFE
1. Papa doesn't have enough money to pay the loan.	In everyday life, many people have financial problems like this. Many people don't have enough money to pay all of their bills.

Pair Discussion   With a partner, compare what you have written in your charts. Correct any mistakes you find. Then discuss what you have written. Do you agree or disagree?

4. Writing

Choose one of the following writing assignments:

1. Write a summary of the story in two to three paragraphs. Be sure to include all the major events.
2. Write an entry in Maud Martha's diary the night she received the good news.
3. Create a dialogue between Maud Martha and Helen the day after Papa receives the extension on his loan.
4. Describe Helen's party.
5. Describe a moment in your life when you expected to hear bad news but things turned out happily.
6. Compare Yuri's mother in "The Bracelet" with Mama in "Home."
7. Compare the problems of the characters in "The Bracelet" with those of the characters in "Home."

Summing Up

A | TAKE A CLOSER LOOK

1. Theme Comparison: Loss

The stories in Part Four all have characters who have to think about loss of one kind or another. Jerry loses an education; Maud Martha is in danger of losing her house; and Mrs. Sandoval loses a child. Think about how the characters in the stories face serious situations that call on them to be strong.

1. How do the characters cope with loss in each of the stories?
2. How does Homer help Mrs. Sandoval?
3. How do Mama, Maud Martha, and Helen help each other?
4. Who helps Jerry?

2. Freewriting

Write the word *war* on the top of a sheet of paper. Then, make a list of words you think of when you see or hear this word. Think of stories you've read and pictures you've seen of war. Then, for fifteen minutes, write about your own feelings when you think of the word *war*.

B | REVIEW

1. Idioms and Expressions Review

The following story will use some of the idioms you learned in Part Four. Work with a partner or in a small group. Fill in the blanks with the correct idioms and expressions. The first letter of each answer is supplied.

sit down with	laid up	sitting pretty	as good as
on account of	dragged on	soft job	come right out and say

When Helen needed advice about a career change, she called her best friend, Sally.

"Sally, I need to s_it_ _down_ _with_ you and talk. Are you free this evening?"

"Sure, Helen. Drop by my place about eight."

As Helen approached Sally's house, she thought of all the good things her friend had done for her. When she was l_____ _____ in bed o_____ _____ _____ the flu and thought she was almost a_____ _____ _____ dead, Sally was there to nurse her back to health.

Sally welcomed Helen. She took her coat and made her sit down. "What's the matter, Helen?" she asked. "C_____ _____ _____ _____ _____ it."

"Well," said Helen, "I want to get a new job. I've d_____ _____ too long in this company. I don't want a s_____ _____. I want an exciting position with new challenges."

Sally thought for a moment. "Helen, you ought to see my brother. He's the personnel manager of ABC Corporation. I'll make an appointment for you with him tomorrow. He'll help you. Before long you'll be s_____ _____."

"Thanks, Sally. I really appreciate it."

2. Form Review

Complete the following sentences by choosing the correct form from the choices in parentheses:

1. Homer stood (awkward, awkwardly) on the steps of Mrs. Sandoval's house.

2. She (sudden, suddenly) appeared at the door.

3. When we get enough sleep, we usually feel very (good, well).

4. Please drive (slow, slowly) on this road. It is very (dangerous, dangerously).

5. Eat some more fruit. You have eaten (hard, hardly) anything.

6. Marissa always speaks (respectful, respectfully) to both her friends and her neighbors.

7. Whenever I am depressed, I try to think (positive, positively).

PART FIVE

Men and Women

Chapter 12

THE WOMAN
– *Zona Gale*

Chapter 13

THE TIGRESS AND
HER MATE
– *James Thurber*

IN FAIRY tales, boy meets girl, they fall in love, and live happily ever after. In real life, love stories may not end happily. Couples don't always marry for love. Sometimes, they marry for money, security, or social position. Many marriages become a "battle between the sexes."

As you read the stories that follow, think of which marriage is the most appealing. What qualities would you want in someone with whom you planned to spend your life?

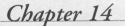 *Chapter 14*

THE KISS
— Kate Chopin

Chapter 12

The Woman ZONA GALE

A PRE-READING

1. Think Before You Read

Answer the following questions:

1. What do you want most in this world?
2. What do you need to be happy?
3. Some people believe you can never be happy if you're poor. What do you think? Give an example from literature or from real life.
4. How do ideas of happiness often change as we grow older?

2. Picture Focus

With a partner, talk about the picture. What do you think is happening?

3. Story Preview

Read the preview of the story and, with a partner, try to guess the meaning of the words in **bold** print.

Bellard walks by a **shabby** house in the suburbs. He is filled with **compassion** for the older man sitting on the porch. But why does the man look so happy?

Bellard's dream of a future as a rich man ends when his father loses his money. Bellard leaves college, gets a job, and marries a girl that he loves.

Bellard and his wife, Lucile, aren't rich, but they are happy. They aren't **dying for** anything that they don't already have. Their children grow up and move away. When Bellard's business fails, his son and daughter return. They **patronize** their parents and become **exasperated** when Bellard and Lucile don't seem worried about their future.

4. Using the Vocabulary

Fill in the blanks below with the **bold** words from the Story Preview above. Then, with a partner, compare your answers.

The house at the end of our street had been empty for a long time, and it was

starting to look very _____shabby_____ . My father was _____

someone to move into the house and fix it up because he loved our neighborhood

and wanted it to look nice. One day, just when Dad was starting to feel

_____ , we saw a moving van pull up in front of the empty house.

My father went outside and started down the street. I decided to join him, saying:

"Dad, I hope you'll show some _____ toward our new neighbors.

Their new house needs a lot of work, but please don't _____ them

by making too many suggestions. Instead, let's find out how we can help." Just

weeks later, it was hard to believe our new neighbors' house was the same one that

had sat empty and abandoned for all those months.

5. *Making Predictions*

From the Story Preview, try to predict what Bellard and Lucile will do. Which of the following predictions do you think is the most *probable?* Circle your choice or give an answer that you think is better.

1. They will go to live with their daughter.

2. They will go to live with their son.

3. They will start a new business and make a lot of money.

4. They will become angry and unhappy.

5. They will continue to be poor but happy.

6. _____

Journal Writing   In your journal, explain why you chose your answer.

IDIOMS AND EXPRESSIONS	
the extreme of the fashion the latest style	**moral crisis** difficult situation that causes one to choose between right and wrong
was torn by noticed, was affected by	
mean little poor-looking	**in all probability** almost definitely
observed the trick of a girl's eyes fell in love	**straighten things out** make everything all right
doing their utmost doing their best	**rose on strong wings** felt encouraged

---

6. *Literary Term: Cause and Effect*

When you read a text, it is important to understand why certain events occur. One event is often the direct result of another. In other words, one thing happens; then, as a result, a second thing happens. The first event is the **cause,** and the next event (or events) is the **effect.**

Focus   As you read "The Woman," think about the cause-and-effect relationships among the events in the story.

About the Author

Zona Gale (1874–1938) was born in Portage, Wisconsin. After she graduated from the University of Wisconsin, she spent five years working as a newspaper reporter in Milwaukee and New York City. In 1904, she returned to her hometown and soon attracted attention as a fiction writer with her early stories of small-town life.

Gale's best-known work, a novel called *Miss Lulu Brett,* gives a realistic view of life in the Midwestern United States in the early twentieth century. The version of *Miss Lulu Brett* that was performed on stage won the Pulitzer Prize in 1921. In many of her novels, short stories, and plays, Gale explores the relationships between men and women, as you will see when you read "The Woman."

The Woman

Walking one day in a suburb, Bellard, wearing clothes in the extreme of the fashion, was torn by the look of a house on whose mean little porch near the street sat a shabby man of sixty, without a coat, and reading a newspaper. The man's fate seemed terrible: the unpainted house, the disordered hall, the glimpse of a woman in an apron. But the man looked up, and smiled at Bellard as brightly as if he himself had been young.

Bellard meant to be a financier. Instead, he shortly endured his father's bankruptcy, left college, found uncongenial employment, observed the trick of a girl's eyes, married her and lived in a little flat.

But this girl had the quality of a flower. Bellard could not explain it, but she was silent and fragrant, and hopeful like a flower. Once in April when he saw a pot of lilies of the valley blooming on the pavement, he thought: "They're like Lucile. They're all doing their utmost." In her presence it was impossible to be discouraged. He would go home from work hating his office, his routine, his fellows, his street; but as soon as he entered the flat, there would be some breath of that air for which he saw other men dying. Her welcome, her abstraction,[1] her silence, her confidences were all really heavenly. Bellard wondered at her, did not comprehend her, adored her. He worked hard, and went home on the subway with a sense of happiness.

He longed to give her beautiful things, but she said: "How do people get like that, my dear – to want expensive things and to have people look up to them? Isn't it foolish?" He wondered how she knew that, and he wished that he knew it himself.

Their two children were like all agreeable children, and Bellard and Lucile went through the reverence, anxiety, and joy of their upbringing. And whether the moment yielded a torn frock or a hurt knee, croup or a moral crisis, Lucile seemed to put the event in its place and not to be overwhelmed by it. "She has a genius for being alive," Bellard thought.

As she grew older, she was not so beautiful, and he saw many women both beautiful and young. But when they chattered, pouted and coquetted,[2] when they were cynical,[3] bored, critical, or hilarious,[4] he thought about Lucile and her silences, her fragrance, her hope. Hope of what? She knew that they would in all probability never have any more than they had now. When he asked her wistfully what kept her so happy she replied with an air of wonder: "You."

One day he overheard her talking about him with a friend. Lucile was saying: "Other men live in things and events and emotions and the future. But he seems to know that living is something else...."
"What else?" this friend interrupted curiously. And he heard Lucile say: "Well, of course every one knows, really. But he lives it too." "I'm not good enough for her," Bellard thought, and tried his best to prove that he was.

They went on like this for years; the children grew up, married, came home and patronized them. Then Bellard, who had established a little business, failed. His son tried to straighten things out, found it impossible, and assumed control, frankly berating his father. His daughter came home with her three children, and filled the flat with clamor and turbulence. This woman said: "Mother, sometimes I think it's your

> *"Other men live in things and events and emotions and the future. But he seems to know that living is something else...."*

[1] *abstraction:* disinterest in worldly things.
[2] *coquetted:* flirted.
[3] *cynical:* doubting the worth of life; sneering and critical.
[4] *hilarious:* extremely gay and noisy.

fault. You're so *patient* with him." "I'm glad he's out of that business," Lucile said absently. "He never liked it." Her exasperated daughter cried: "But what are you going to live on?" Bellard heard her say: "Your father was responsible for three of us for a quarter of a century, you know, dear." At this Bellard rose on strong wings and felt himself still able to breast the morning and the night.[5]

Lucile and Bellard moved to a suburb. There they rented a little house and Bellard went into a real estate office. All day he showed land and houses to men who wanted something better for less money. At night he went home and there was Lucile – less like a flower, but still silent, fragrant, hopeful. He said to her: "You'll never have anything more than you have now, Lucile, do you realize that?" She replied: "I don't want anything more to dust and take care of!" Once he said: "When you were a girl you dreamed that you'd have things different, didn't you, Lucile?" She said:

"My dear, all that poor girl knew how to dream was just about having things!" He cried: "What do you want most of anything in this world?" She considered and answered: "I want you to be as happy as I am."

He thought of his own early dream of being a great financier, and said: "I'm the happy one, you know." He thought: "This is what the world is dying for."

One day, when he was sixty, he was sitting on his mean little porch near the street. The house was small and unpainted, the hall was disordered with house cleaning, Lucile in an apron was in the doorway. Bellard, without a coat and reading a newspaper, lifted his eyes, and saw walking by the house, and wearing clothes in the extreme of the fashion, a youth who looked up at him with an excess of visible compassion.

On this youth Bellard looked down and smiled, a luminous smile, a smile as bright as if he himself had been young.

[5] *breast the morning and the night:* confront challenges energetically and optimistically.

1. Understanding the Story

With a partner, answer these questions.

1. Why does the young Bellard pity the older man he saw sitting on the porch?
2. What event changes Bellard's plans for the future?
3. How does Lucile make Bellard happy? What did she want most in this world?
4. How do Bellard's children react when his business fails? Who does his daughter blame for the failure? Why?
5. How does the story end? Is it a happy or a sad ending? Why?

2. Vocabulary Comprehension

Read each of the following sentences. Then circle the letter of the answer that gives the correct meaning for each word in **bold** print.

1. Bellard felt bad for the man on the porch because his **fate** seemed terrible.
   a. religious beliefs
   b. future
   c. living arrangements
   d. physical appearance

2. The house in the suburbs was unpainted and **disordered.**
   a. ugly
   b. made of wood
   c. messy
   d. dirty

3. He wanted to become a **financier** after college.
   a. businessperson
   b. architect
   c. lawyer
   d. engineer

4. He found an **uncongenial** job.
   a. low-paying
   b. exciting
   c. difficult
   d. unpleasant

5. Lucile was **fragrant,** like a flower.
   a. delicate
   b. beautiful
   c. sweet-smelling
   d. colorful

6. Bellard thought Lucile was a **heavenly** woman.
   a. religious
   c. happy
   b. intelligent
   d. wonderful

7. Even after twenty-five years, Bellard didn't **comprehend** his wife.
   a. understand
   c. believe
   b. know
   d. think about

8. He **longed** to give his wife beautiful things.
   a. tried
   c. wanted
   b. worked hard
   d. liked

9. It's terrible when parents **berate** their children and even worse when children **berate** their parents.
   a. hit
   c. ignore
   b. leave
   d. criticize

10. There is usually quite a bit of **clamor and turbulence** in a children's playground.
    a. noise and confusion
    c. fun and games
    b. crying and screaming
    d. happiness and friendship

11. Lucile **considered** Bellard's question and then gave him an answer that any husband would want to hear.
    a. listened to
    c. repeated
    b. thought about
    d. waited for

12. Lucile was always **patient** with Bellard.
    a. distant
    c. loving, tender
    b. sweet
    d. calm, uncomplaining

13. Bellard **was responsible for** his family for a quarter of a century.
    a. helped
    c. was nice to
    b. took care of
    d. thought about

14. Lucile was never **overwhelmed** by events.
    a. made anxious
    c. made powerless
    b. made to cry
    d. made angry

3. Word Forms

Complete the chart by filling in the various forms of the following words taken from "The Woman." An X indicates that no form is possible. Use your dictionary if you need help. **Note:** There may be more than one possible word for the same part of speech.

Verb	Noun	Adjective	Adverb
criticize	*criticism*		
consider			
X		patient	
		silent	
X	fragrance		
		bright	
X	anxiety		
	bankruptcy		X

Work with a partner. Write sentence groups using as many related word forms from the chart as possible.

> *Example:*
> Some parents are very **critical** of their children. They seem to **criticize** everything their children do. This kind of **criticism** can be very hurtful.

4. Grammar: Possessive Nouns

> **A possessive singular noun is formed by adding 's.**
>
> *Examples:*
> the man's fate
> a girl's eyes

If the singular noun ends in -*s*, the possessive is formed in two possible ways: by adding *'s* or by adding only an apostrophe (').

Examples:
Dickens's novels *or* Dickens' novels
James's house *or* James' house

A plural noun ending in -*s* is made possessive by adding only an apostrophe ('). However, irregular plural forms that don't end in -*s* require *'s*.

Examples:
the lilies' fragrance
her two friends' children
the men's room
the people's problem

5. Application

Reread the story to look for examples of possessive nouns. Then join the following pairs of nouns to make possessive noun forms:

1. porch/Bellard _____ *Bellard's porch* _____

2. toys/the children _____

3. apartment/Frances _____

4. apron/Lucile _____

5. school/the boys _____

6. characters/Dickens _____

7. speech/the President _____

8. wife/Charles _____

9. lounge/the teachers _____

10. restroom/the women _____

11. property/your parents _____

12. civil rights/people _____

1. Sharing Ideas

Discuss the following questions with a partner or in a group:

1. What does Bellard mean when he describes Lucile as "silent and fragrant, and hopeful like a flower"?
2. Does Lucile understand her husband? What does she say about him to her friend? to her children?
3. What's your opinion of Bellard and Lucile's children? Were you surprised that they acted the way they did? What do you think the author's attitude is toward these two characters?
4. Why did the author use almost the exact same words to begin and end the story? Do you think it was a good idea? Did it make the story easier to understand? Why or why not?
5. Why do you think Zona Gale named the story "A Woman"? Can you think of two other titles that the author could have used instead?

2. Reading Between the Lines

Practice reading between the lines. Circle the letter of the best answer.

1. In talking about her husband, Lucile said, "But he seems to know that living is something else. . . ." We can assume Lucile meant that Bellard
   a. didn't understand life.
   b. knew what was most important in life.
   c. wanted to die.

2. Bellard said Lucile "has a genius for being alive" because he thought she
   a. knew how to enjoy life.
   b. took good care of herself.
   c. was very intelligent.

3. Imagine that Zona Gale wrote "The Woman" as a fable, which is a short story that teaches a moral. What's the lesson of the story?
   a. Fate determines our future.
   b. A lack of ambition can result in poverty.
   c. Love, not success, brings happiness.

3. Analyzing the Story

Look back at the Literary Term on page 160. Think of some examples of cause-and-effect relationships in this story. Then fill in the missing cause or effect in the following chart. The first one has been done for you.

CAUSE	EFFECT
1. Bellard's father went bankrupt.	1. *Bellard had to quit college and find a job.*
2.	2. Bellard went home from work with a sense of happiness.
3. Lucile grew older.	3.
4.	4. He thought about Lucile.
5. Bellard thought he wasn't good enough for Lucile.	5.
6.	6. His son took over.
7. Their daughter came home with her three children.	7.
8.	8. Bellard smiled at him.

Pair Discussion   With a partner, compare what you have written in your charts. Correct any mistakes you find. Discuss what you have written.

4. Writing

Choose one of the following writing assignments:

1. Write a summary of the story in two to three paragraphs. Be sure to include all the major events. Look at the cause-and-effect chart above if you need help.
2. Do you know anyone like Bellard or Lucile? Write a character description of that person.
3. How do you think Bellard's life would have been different if he had become a successful financier? Write a new version of "The Woman" in two to three paragraphs, telling what his life would have been like as a wealthy man.

Chapter 13

The Tigress and Her Mate JAMES THURBER

1. *Think Before You Read*

Answer the following questions:

1. Think about married couples that you know or have read about. What must people do to have a good marriage? Now describe a bad marriage.
2. In your opinion, should fathers spend as much time with their children as mothers do? Why or why not?
3. The author of "The Tigress and Her Mate," James Thurber, liked to write about absurd (or silly) situations. Describe an absurd situation that you've experienced or read about.

2. Picture Focus

With a partner, talk about the picture. What do you think is happening?

3. Story Preview

Read the preview of the story and, with a partner, try to guess the meaning of the words in **bold** print.

In this story, Sabra and Proudfoot are tigers who talk and behave like human beings. A short time after Proudfoot and Sabra **set up housekeeping,** Proudfoot gets tired of his **mate.** Soon he is being **mean** to her and spending less and less time at home.

One day Sabra tells Proudfoot that she is pregnant, but he isn't at all glad. Instead, he leaves and doesn't come home until after the **blessed event.** When Proudfoot threatens to **drown** the children if they disturb his sleep, Sabra decides she has had enough.

4. Using the Vocabulary

Fill in the blanks below with the **bold** words from the Story Preview above. Then, with a partner, compare your answers.

From the minute they met, Dora and Mike knew that they had found their

perfect _____*mate*_____. Two years later, they got married and

_____. As with so many married couples, there were good times

but there were also angry moments when they would say _____

things to each other.

   One night, Dora told Mike that they were going to have a baby. Such

wonderful news! After the _____ , their lives were never the same.

A child brings joy and happiness, and as any parent can tell you, a child also

brings worry and fear. How many parents lie awake at night thinking of ways to

protect their children, worrying that they will _____ in deep water

or be hit by a car?

5. Making Predictions

From the Story Preview, try to predict what will happen between Proudfoot and Sabra. Which of the following predictions do you think is the most *probable?* Circle your choice or give an answer that you think is better.

1. Proudfoot will leave Sabra for another tigress.

2. Sabra will teach Proudfoot to be a good husband and father.

3. Proudfoot will hurt his family.

4. Sabra will raise her cubs without Proudfoot.

5. _____

Journal Writing   In your journal, explain why you chose your answer. Then read the story.

IDIOMS AND EXPRESSIONS	
fell to started to **What the hell's the matter with you?** What in the world is wrong with you? **Forget it.** Stop thinking about it. **Hush.** Be quiet. **the chosen species** humans **take place** happen	**plainclothes** regular clothing that some police officers wear on duty **prowl car** police car **hit the sack** go to bed **Scat.** Go away. **was nailed** was hit **right cross** a boxing term for using the right fist to punch someone

6. Literary Term: Fable

A **fable** is a short story with a moral, or a lesson. The characters in fables are often animals who speak and act like humans. The most famous fables were written by Aesop, a Greek slave living in the sixth century B.C. Another famous writer of fables was the seventeenth century French author La Fontaine.

Focus   As you read "The Tigress and Her Mate," think about why the author probably chose to use animals instead of people to tell his story.

About the Author

James Thurber (1894–1961) was born and raised in Columbus, Ohio. After working for several newspapers, he was a staff writer for *The New Yorker* magazine from 1927 to 1933 and later regularly contributed stories, anecdotes, and cartoons to the magazine until his death.

Because of his talent for wit and irony, James Thurber is considered one of America's greatest humorists. His stories often deal with middle-class domestic issues and conflicts between men and women. Thurber enjoyed taking serious situations and making them funny, as you will see when you read "The Tigress and Her Mate."

The Tigress and Her Mate

Proudfoot, a tiger, became tired of his mate, Sabra, a few weeks after they had set up
5 housekeeping, and he fell to leaving home earlier and earlier in the morning, and returning later and later at night. He no longer called her "Sugar Paw," or anything else, but
10 merely clapped his paws when he wanted anything, or, if she was upstairs, whistled. The last long speech he ever made to her at breakfast was "What the hell's the matter with you? I
15 bring you rice and peas and coconut oil, don't I? Love is something you put away in the attic with your wedding dress. Forget it." And he finished his coffee, put down the *Jungle News,* and started for the door. 20

"Where are you going?" Sabra asked.

"Out," he said. And after that, every time she asked him where he was going, he said "Out," or "Away," or "Hush." 25

When Sabra became aware of the coming of what would have been, had she belonged to the chosen species, a blessed event, and told Proudfoot about it, he snarled, "Growp." He had 30 now learned to talk to his mate in code, and "growp" meant "I hope the cubs grow up to be xylophone players or major generals." Then he went away, as all male tigers do at such a moment, for he did not want to be bothered by his young until the males were old enough to box with and the females old enough to insult. While waiting for the unblessed event to take place, he spent his time fighting water buffaloes and riding around with plainclothes tigers in a prowl car.

When he finally came home, he said to his mate, "Eeps," meaning "I'm going to hit the sack, and if the kids keep me awake by yowling, I'll drown them like so many common house kittens." Sabra stalked to the front door of their house,

▪ ▪ ▪

Sabra stalked to the front door of their house, opened it, and said to her mate, "Scat."

▪ ▪ ▪

opened it, and said to her mate, "Scat." The fight that took place was terrible but brief. Proudfoot led with the wrong paw, was nailed with the swiftest right cross in the jungle, and never really knew where he was after that. The next morning, when the cubs, male and female, tumbled eagerly down the stairs demanding to know what they could do, their mother said, "You can go in the parlor and play with your father. He's the tiger rug just in front of the fireplace. I hope you'll like him."

The children loved him.

MORAL: *Never be mean to a tiger's wife, especially if you're the tiger.*

1. *Understanding the Story*

With a partner, answer these questions.

1. Why does Proudfoot leave the house early and come home late?
2. How does Proudfoot's behavior toward Sabra change? How does he speak to her?
3. What is Proudfoot's reaction to Sabra's announcement that they are going to be parents? What does Proudfoot wish for his children's future?
4. What part of his children's lives does Proudfoot want to miss?
5. What does Proudfoot say to Sabra that makes her very angry? How does their fight begin? How does it end?
6. Explain the last sentence of the story, "The children loved him."

2. *Vocabulary Comprehension*

Read each of the following sentences. Then circle the letter of the answer that gives the correct meaning for each word in **bold** print.

1. Instead of speaking to Sabra, Proudfoot **merely** clapped his paws when he wanted something.
   a. loudly
   b. only
   c. quickly
   d. impatiently

2. I called my friend the minute I **became aware** that she was sick.
   a. thought
   b. was afraid
   c. knew
   d. felt

3. What should you do when a dog **snarls** at you?
   a. makes an angry sound
   b. bites
   c. licks
   d. jumps

4. During a war, military instructions are often written in **code.**
   a. a foreign language
   b. small letters
   c. a secret language
   d. musical notes

5. It isn't difficult to learn to play the **xylophone.**
   a. a sport
   b. a game
   c. a trick
   d. a musical instrument

6. After many years in the U.S. Air Force, he became a **major general.**
   a. a high-ranking officer   c. a middle-ranking soldier
   b. a pilot   d. an important retired person

7. Some parents teach their children to **box** so that they can defend themselves.
   a. fight with one's hands   c. run long distances
   b. become strong   d. stay calm

8. The **yowling** cat kept me awake most of the night.
   a. meowing   c. crying
   b. active   d. snarling

3. Word Forms

Complete the chart by filling in the various forms of the following words taken from "The Tigress and Her Mate." An X indicates that no form is possible. Use your dictionary if you need help. **Note:** There may be more than one possible word for the same part of speech.

VERB	NOUN	ADJECTIVE	ADVERB
_____	*length*	long	X
insult	_____	_____	_____
X	_____	terrible	_____
X	_____	_____	eagerly
X	_____	mean	_____
X	_____	swift	_____

Work with a partner. Write sentence groups with the words in the chart, using as many related word forms as possible. Your sentences can be related to the story "The Tigress and Her Mate," but they don't have to be.

> *Example:*
> I don't like the length of these pants. They aren't long enough, so I'm going to lengthen them. It won't take long.

4. Grammar: Comparative Adjectives and Adverbs

The comparative of one-syllable adjectives and adverbs is formed by adding *-er*.

Examples:

Proudfoot came home late on Friday, but he came home even later on Saturday.

Proudfoot was swift, but his mate was much swifter.

Yesterday was so cold that I thought I would freeze, but today the weather feels a little warmer.

The comparative of most two-syllable adjectives and adverbs, especially those ending in *-y,* is formed by adding *-er*.

Example:

Proudfoot left early on Monday, but he left even earlier on Tuesday.

When we sat down to dinner I was hungry, and seeing the delicious food made me even hungrier.

Speaking a foreign language is difficult at first, but the more you do it, the easier it becomes.

The comparative of other two-syllable and longer adjectives and adverbs is formed with *more*.

Examples:

Sabra was more interested in the cubs than Proudfoot was.

Sabra took parenthood more seriously than Proudfoot did.

I was thinking about buying my mother jewelry for her birthday, but I'd really rather get her something more unusual.

Most students go out more often on the weekend than during the week when they have to study.

Some adjectives and adverbs have an irregular comparative form.

good/well	better
bad/badly	worse

Examples:

James is a good student, but his brother is better.

James does well in school, but his brother does better.

Kathy is a bad singer, but her sister is worse.

Kathy sings badly but her sister sings worse.

5. Application

Complete the following sentences with the correct comparative form of the adjective or adverb in parentheses:

1. (good/expensive)   The food at Rico's Restaurant is _____*better*_____ than the food at Cathy's Café, but it's also __*more expensive*__ .

2. (cloudy/hot)   Today is _____ than yesterday, and it's _____ too.

3. (beautiful/dangerous)   Some people think tigers are _____ than lions. Do you think that tigers are _____?

4. (pretty/intelligent)   Jenny is very pretty, but I think May is even _____. She's also _____.

5. (exciting)   Tonight's game was much _____ than last night's game.

6. (close/well)   The score tonight was _____ , and the players played _____.

7. (difficult/poor)   In some countries, it's _____ than ever for people to find work, so they become _____ every day.

8. (bad)   Your handwriting has gotten _____.
   (carelessly) You write even _____ than you did before.

9. (short)   The barber cut your hair _____ this time.
   (good/long) I think it looks _____ when it's a little _____.

10. (important)   Is it _____ to make a lot of money or to be happy?

1. Sharing Ideas

Discuss the following questions with a partner or in a group:

1. How does Thurber mix animal traits with human characteristics? Give examples from the story.
2. What kind of mate is Proudfoot? Do you know anyone like him?
3. Who do you feel sorry for at the end of the story? Why?
4. Explain how Thurber took a serious situation and made it funny. Give examples of how the story might have been sad and tragic if the author had written it differently.

2. Reading Between the Lines

Practice reading between the lines. Complete the following tasks:

1. Proudfoot seems to think that his only role in his marriage is to bring home food for the family to eat. Find the lines in the story that show this.

2. The story never says that Proudfoot has a job, but we can assume that he works. What is his occupation? Circle the best answer. Then find the lines in the story that support your answer.
   a. chef
   b. soldier
   c. police officer

3. Although there is no detailed description of Proudfoot and Sabra's home, we can conclude that the house has more than one floor or story. Find two places in the story that show that the house probably has three floors.

4. In the story, Thurber seems to be expressing an opinion. How did the author probably feel about families? Circle the best answer.
   a. It's better for children to grow up with two parents than with only one.
   b. It's worse for children to grow up with a bad father than to have no father at all.
   c. Mothers are more important than fathers.

5. The story never says that Sabra kills Proudfoot, but we can assume she did. Find the line that proves that Proudfoot is dead.

3. Analyzing the Story

Look back at the Literary Term on page 172. Think of how the story would have been different if Thurber hadn't used animals as characters. Change one or more words from the following parts of the story so that the phrases describe people – and not tigers. The first one has been done for you.

ANIMALS	HUMANS
1. Proudfoot became tired of his mate.	*Peter became tired of his wife.*
2. merely clapped his paws	
3. put down the *Jungle News*	
4. I hope the cubs grow up.	
5. He spent his time fighting water buffaloes.	
6. riding around with plainclothes tigers	
7. Proudfoot led with the wrong paw.	
8. when the cubs tumbled eagerly down the stairs	

Now answer this question:

How would the story probably have ended if the characters had been humans?

_____

_____

_____

_____

Pair Discussion   With a partner, compare what you have written in your charts. Correct any mistakes you find. Discuss your answer to the question above with your partner.

4. Writing

Choose one of the following writing assignments:

1. Write a summary of the story in two to three paragraphs. Make sure to include all the major events. Look back at the story if you need help.
2. Write a fable. Your story may be humorous or serious, but it must have animal characters and a moral.
3. Read another fable, either one by Aesop or La Fontaine, or another by James Thurber. Write a two- to three-paragraph summary of the fable, including the moral.
4. Imagine that Sabra remarries. What kind of tiger does she marry? How does her new husband treat her and her children? Is her new mate a good husband and a good stepfather? Write a story about Sabra and her children's new life.

Chapter 14
The Kiss KATE CHOPIN

PRE-READING

1. Think Before You Read

Answer the following questions:

1. What are some reasons why people marry? What are some of their reasons for choosing the partner they choose?
2. Do you think it's all right for people to marry for money? Why or why not?
3. Do you that think people who are in love tend to see the person they love clearly? Why or why not?

2. Picture Focus

With a partner, talk about the picture. What do you think is happening?

3. Story Preview

Read the preview of the story and, with a partner, try to guess the meaning of the words in **bold** print.

Brantain is visiting Nathalie. He is rather **unattractive;** she is very beautiful. He is very honest about his feelings. From the **ardent** way he looks at her, it's very obvious that he is in love. He plans to ask her to marry him, and marriage is what Nathalie wants as well. But Nathalie is full of **guile.** She doesn't love Brantain, but he is rich and Nathalie wants the kind of life that money could give her.

Suddenly, the door opens, and a second young man, Harvy, comes in. Harvy is a friend of Nathalie's brother, and he is evidently on **intimate** terms with Nathalie. Not seeing Brantain, he walks over to Nathalie and plants an ardent kiss on her lips. Brantain jumps up and leaves, confused and upset. Harvy is also confused and upset. Nathalie is angry. Has her plan been ruined, or can she save it?

4. Using the Vocabulary

Fill in the blanks below with the **bold** words from the Story Preview above. Then, with a partner, compare your answers.

In the years before women could have money and careers of their own, women had to depend on finding the right husband. Girls were told that they should not let a man know their real feelings, because he might lose interest. A(n)

_____*ardent*_____ look in your eye might send the man running – or might make him think he could kiss you without marrying you. _____

behavior, like holding hands or even sitting close together, could make people think badly of you. A beautiful woman had an advantage over a woman who was

_____. But any woman could use _____ ; after all,

there were many ways to influence or even trick a man.

5. Making Predictions

From the Story Preview, try to predict what will happen. Which of the following predictions do you think is the most *probable?* Circle your choice or give an answer that you think is better.

1. Nathalie will marry Brantain but keep seeing Harvy.

2. She will marry Brantain and lose Harvy.

3. She will try to marry Brantain but fail, losing both men.

4. She will realize that Harvy is her true love and marry him.

5. She will try to marry Harvy but discover that he is no longer interested.

6. _____

Journal Writing   In your journal, explain why you chose your answer.

IDIOMS AND EXPRESSIONS	
send a slow glance* look at someone	**presence of mind** calmness and self-control in a difficult situation
seek someone's society* try to be with someone	**What's the matter?** What's the problem?
declare oneself* propose marriage	**uncalled for** not necessary

*Today, these expressions would be considered literary; they would not commonly be used in conversation.

6. Literary Term: Irony

In literature **irony** frequently occurs when there is a difference between what is expected or desired and what actually happens. For example, what a character thinks will happen to him or her may turn out to be the exact opposite of what actually does happen.

Focus   After you read "The Kiss," ask yourself whether there were differences between what characters expected and wanted, and what happened.

About the Author

Kate Chopin (1851–1904) was born Katherine O'Flaherty in St. Louis, Missouri. At nineteen, she married Oscar Chopin, a Louisiana planter. When he died in 1882, leaving her in debt, Kate supported her six children by writing stories. Although her marriage had been happy, as a widow, she enjoyed her freedom and the popularity she achieved through her writing. In thirteen years, Chopin wrote nearly 100 stories, poems, and essays. The stories often deal with misunderstood women trapped in unhappy marriages. "The Kiss," as you'll see, is an exception.

The Kiss

It was still quite light out of doors, but inside with the curtains drawn and the smouldering fire sending out a dim,
5 uncertain glow, the room was full of deep shadows.

Brantain sat in one of these shadows; it had overtaken him and he
10 did not mind. The obscurity lent him courage to keep his eyes fastened as ardently as he liked upon the girl who sat in the firelight.

She was very handsome, with a
15 certain fine, rich coloring that belongs to the healthy brune[1] type. She was quite composed, as she idly stroked the satiny coat of the cat that lay curled in her lap, and she occasionally sent a slow glance into the shadow 20 where her companion sat. They were talking low, of indifferent things which plainly were not the things that occupied their thoughts. She knew that he loved her – a frank, blustering 25 fellow without guile enough to conceal his feelings, and no desire to do so. For two weeks past he had sought[2] her society eagerly and persistently. She was confidently waiting for him to 30 declare himself and she meant to accept him. The rather insignificant[3] and unattractive Brantain was enormously rich; and she liked and

---

[1] *brune:* brunette; having brown or black hair.

[2] *sought:* past form of *seek.*

[3] *insignificant:* not impressive in appearance.

required the entourage[4] which wealth could give her.

During one of the pauses between their talk of the last tea and the next reception[5] the door opened and a young man entered whom Brantain knew quite well. The girl turned her face toward him. A stride or two brought him to her side, and bending over her chair – before she could suspect his intention, for she did not realize that he had not seen her visitor – he pressed an ardent, lingering kiss upon her lips.

Brantain slowly arose; so did the girl arise, but quickly, and the newcomer stood between them, a little amusement and some defiance struggling with the confusion in his face.

"I believe," stammered Brantain, "I see that I have stayed too long. I – I had no idea – that is, I must wish you good-bye." He was clutching his hat with both hands, and probably did not perceive that she was extending her hand to him, her presence of mind had not completely deserted her; but she could not have trusted herself to speak.

"Hang me if I saw him sitting there,[6] Nattie! I know it's deuced awkward[7] for you. But I hope you'll forgive me this once – this very first break.[8] Why, what's the matter?"

"Don't touch me; don't come near me," she returned angrily. "What do you mean by entering the house without ringing?"

"I came in with your brother, as I often do," he answered coldly, in self-justification. "We came in the side way. He went upstairs and I came in here hoping to find you. The explanation is simple enough and ought to satisfy you that the misadventure was unavoidable. But do say that you forgive me, Nathalie," he entreated, softening.

"Forgive you! You don't know what you are talking about. Let me pass. It depends upon – a good deal whether I ever forgive you."

At that next reception which she and Brantain had been talking about she approached the young man with a delicious frankness of manner when she saw him there.

"Will you let me speak to you a moment or two, Mr. Brantain?" she asked with an engaging but perturbed smile. He seemed extremely unhappy; but when she took his arm and walked away with him, seeking a retired corner, a ray of hope mingled with the almost comical misery of his expression. She was apparently very outspoken.

"Perhaps I should not have sought this interview, Mr. Brantain; but – but, oh, I have been very uncomfortable, almost miserable since that little

[4] *entourage:* surroundings and people around one.
[5] *tea, reception:* two kinds of parties.
[6] *Hang me if I saw him sitting there:* strong way of saying he didn't see him.
[7] *deuced awkward:* very awkward.
[8] *first break:* first time he's not acted in the right way.

encounter the other afternoon. When I thought how you might have misinterpreted it, and believed things" – hope was plainly gaining the ascendancy over misery in Brantain's round, guileless face – "of course, I know it is nothing to you, but for my own sake I do want you to understand that Mr. Harvy is an intimate friend of long standing. Why, we have always been like cousins – like brother and sister, I may say. He is my brother's most intimate associate and often fancies that he is entitled to the same privileges as the family. Oh, I know it is absurd, uncalled for, to tell you this; undignified even," she was almost weeping, "but it makes so much difference to me what you think of – of me." Her voice had grown very low and agitated. The misery had all disappeared from Brantain's face.

"Then you do really care what I think, Miss Nathalie? May I call you Miss Nathalie?" They turned into a long, dim corridor that was lined on either side with tall, graceful plants. They walked slowly to the very end of it. When they turned to retrace their steps Brantain's face was radiant and hers was triumphant.

Harvy was among the guests at the wedding; and he sought her out in a rare moment when she stood alone.

"Your husband," he said, smiling, "has sent me over to kiss you."

A quick blush suffused her face and round polished throat. "I suppose it's natural for a man to feel and act generously on an occasion of this kind. He tells me he doesn't want his marriage to interrupt wholly that pleasant intimacy which has existed between you and me. I don't know what you've been telling him," with an insolent smile, "but he has sent me here to kiss you."

She felt like a chess player who, by the clever handling of his pieces, sees the game taking the course intended. Her eyes were bright and tender with a smile as they glanced up into his; and her lips looked hungry for the kiss which they invited.

"But, you know," he went on quietly, "I didn't tell him so, it would have seemed ungrateful, but I can tell you. I've stopped kissing women; it's dangerous."

Well, she had Brantain and his million left. A person can't have everything in this world; and it was a little unreasonable of her to expect it.

1. Understanding the Story

With a partner, answer these questions.

1. What does Nathalie think of Brantain?
2. Why does she want to marry him?
3. Who is Harvy? How does he cause Nathalie embarrassment and almost ruin her plan?
4. How does Nathalie react to this incident?
5. How does Nathalie get Brantain to propose?
6. At the wedding, what reason does Harvy give for coming over to Nathalie?
7. How does she feel when she thinks he is going to kiss her?
8. Why doesn't he kiss her?

2. Vocabulary Comprehension

Read the following sentences from the story. Then circle the letter of the answer that gives the correct meaning for the words in **bold** print.

1. She was quite **composed,** as she idly stroked the satiny coat of the cat that lay curled in her lap. . . .
   a. calm
   b. nervous
   c. frightened
   d. tired

2. [Brantain was] a **frank,** blustering fellow **without guile** enough to conceal his feelings. . . .
   a. plain-looking . . . not handsome
   b. shy . . . not talkative
   c. sincere . . . not tricky
   d. smart . . . not stupid

3. Bending over her chair . . . he pressed an **ardent, lingering** kiss upon her lips.
   a. full of feeling, lasting awhile
   b. short, quick
   c. friendly, kindly
   d. secret, meant to not be seen

4. He was clutching his hat with both hands, and probably did not **perceive** that she was extending her hand to him. . . .

   a. notice
   b. care
   c. show that he knew
   d. become angry

5. "Will you let me speak to you a moment or two, Mr. Brantain?" she asked with an **engaging** but **perturbed** smile.

   a. angry . . . unfriendly
   b. attractive . . . worried
   c. familiar . . . expected
   d. happy . . . sincere

6. He seemed extremely unhappy; but when she took his arm . . . a ray of hope mingled with the almost comical **misery** of his expression.

   a. great happiness
   b. hopefulness
   c. great unhappiness
   d. good humor

7. "Oh, I know it is **absurd,** uncalled for, to tell you this; **undignified** even," she was almost weeping, "but it makes so much difference to me what you think of – of me."

   a. very silly . . . not appropriate
   b. important . . . not possible to avoid
   c. obvious . . . not surprising
   d. confusing . . . not kind

8. "I don't know what you've been telling him," [he said] with an **insolent** smile, "but he has sent me here to kiss you."

   a. bold, almost rude
   b. gentle, kind
   c. small, unhappy
   d. loving

3. Word Forms

Complete the chart by filling in the various forms of the following words taken from "The Kiss." An X indicates that no form is possible. Use your dictionary if you need help. **Note:** There may be more than one possible word for the same part of speech.

VERB	NOUN	ADJECTIVE	ADVERB
_____	defiance	_defiant_	_____
_____	glow	_____	_____
_____	_____	radiant	_____
_____	_____	agitated	_____
X	_____	insolent	_____
perceive	_____	_____	_____

With a partner, write sentences using some of the word forms above.

4. Grammar: Uses of the Verb Do

In addition to its use as a main verb, *do* is used to form questions and negatives. *Do* is also used as an auxiliary verb. If a sentence does not include the verb *be* or an auxiliary verb (*be, have,* or modal), include *do* to:

show emphasis

Example:
"Then you do really care what I think, Miss Nathalie?"
("Then you really care what I think, Miss Nathalie?" but with more emphasis)

avoid repeating a verb phrase

Example:
[He was] a frank, blustering fellow without guile enough to conceal his feelings, and no desire to do so.
(*do* + *so* = "to conceal his feelings")

5. Application

Identify the use of *do* in each of the following sentences from the story. Write the correct use of *do* on the line below each sentence. Choose one: *to form a question, to form a negative, to show emphasis,* or *to avoid repetition.* The first sentence has been done for you.

1. He . . . probably did not perceive that she was extending her hand to him. . . .

   to form the negative

2. "Don't touch me; don't come near me. . . ."

   _____

3. "What do you mean by entering the house without ringing?"

   _____

4. "I came in with your brother, as I often do. . . ."

   _____

5. "But do say that you forgive me, Nathalie. . . ."

   _____

6. "I do want you to understand that Mr. Harvy is an intimate friend of long standing."

   _____

7. "I didn't tell him so . . . but I can tell you."

   _____

With a partner, write a dialogue between a man and a woman having an argument. The dialogue can be between two of the people in the story or between any two people. Use *do* at least once as a main verb, in questions, in negatives, for emphasis, and to avoid repetition.

D | THINKING ABOUT THE STORY

1. *Sharing Ideas*

Discuss the following questions with a partner or in a group:

1. What are some examples of Nathalie's cleverness?
2. Do you think Harvy and Nathalie are in love with each other? Why or why not?
3. What is your opinion of Brantain? Do you see him as Nathalie does? Do you like him? Do you respect him? Explain.
4. At the end of the story, how does Harvy have "the last word"?
5. The last paragraph implies that Nathalie doesn't really care that she has lost Harvy. Is this what Nathalie would like to think, or does she really feel this way?

2. *Reading Between the Lines*

Practice reading between the lines. Circle the letter of the answer that best completes each of the following statements:

1. In the beginning,
   a. both Brantain and Nathalie seem very confident that they will soon be married.
   b. only Brantain seems very confident that he and Nathalie will soon be married.
   c. only Nathalie seems very confident that she and Brantain will soon be married.

2. When Brantain leaves after the kiss, he is probably most upset because he now feels that Nathalie
   a. is in love with Harvy and won't marry him (Brantain).
   b. is not the kind of person he would want to marry.
   c. is being treated badly by Harvy.

3. After the kiss, Harvy apologizes to Nathalie for
   a. being in love with her.
   b. embarrassing her by kissing her in front of someone else.
   c. ruining her plan by kissing her in front of Brantain.

4. At the wedding, Harvy refuses to kiss Nathalie because
   a. he is angry with her and wants to teach her a lesson.
   b. he is worried about what other people at the wedding would think.
   c. he is in love with another woman and isn't interested in Nathalie anymore.

3. Analyzing the Story

Look back at the Literary Term on page 184 and think about what the three characters in the story want or expect, and what actually happens to them. Make a chart like the one below and fill in your answers.

Scene	What Does the Character Want or Expect?	Is the Result What the Character Wants or Expects?
Conversation between Brantain and Nathalie (lines 21–36)	Brantain: Nathalie:	Brantain: Nathalie:
The kiss (lines 37–86)	Harvy: *to have an intimate moment with Nathalie and make her happy*	Harvy:
The encounter between Harvy and Nathalie at the wedding (lines 136–164)	Nathalie: Harvy:	Nathalie: Harvy:

Pair Discussion Compare charts with a partner. If the result is not what the character wants or expects, how is it different? Irony can also occur when there is a difference between what a character thinks is true about a situation or another character and what the reader knows is true. Can you think of any examples of this kind of irony in the story?

4. Writing

Choose one of the following writing assignments:

1. Write a summary of the story in two to three paragraphs. Be sure to include all the major events. Look at the chart above if you need help.
2. Describe Nathalie's wedding. Pretend that you are writing about the wedding for a newspaper or that you were a guest and are writing a letter to a friend.
3. Write Nathalie's diary entry the day before her wedding. Write another diary entry a week later.
4. Could this story take place today? Why or why not?

Summing Up

1. Theme Comparison: Marriage

People marry for different reasons. Once married, couples do not all behave in the same way. Think about the three very different styles of marriage in the stories and answer the following questions:

1. How do Lucile and Nathalie differ in their attitudes toward their husbands?
2. How do Bellard and Proudfoot differ in their attitudes toward their wives?
3. Sabra is abused by her mate. Is there any other character in the stories who is abused by a mate? Who? In what way?

2. Freewriting

Write the word *marriage* on the top of a sheet of paper. Now, write any words that come into your mind when you think of this word. For fifteen minutes, write your ideas about marriage.

| B | REVIEW |

1. Idioms and Expressions Review

The following story will use some of the idioms you learned in Part Five. Work with a partner or in a small group. Fill in the blanks with the correct idioms and expressions. The first letter of each answer is supplied.

extreme of the fashion	uncalled for	what's the matter?
take place	forget it	presence of mind
torn by	hit the sack	mean little

John fell in love with his co-worker, Jean, because she was intelligent and fun to be with. She was attractive and dressed well, but never in the e _xtreme_ ___of___ ___the___ ___fashion___ . John and Jean dated for almost a year, but John was shy about asking her to be his wife. Finally, Jean had the p_____ _____ _____ to bring the conversation around to the subject of marriage. John became so nervous that Jean said, "W_____ _____ _____?" John realized that his nervousness was u_____ _____ and proposed. To his delight, Jean accepted his proposal although she was t_____ _____ the desire to concentrate on her career.

They decided that their marriage would t_____ _____ as soon as they could find a place to live. They searched for days until they were so tired that all they could do at night was h_____ _____ _____. They continued to search, but they only saw places with m_____ _____ kitchens. Jean became so upset that she got angry with John. Afterwards, she felt terrible. When she apologized, John smiled and said, "F_____ _____." The next day they found an apartment.

2. Form Review

Complete the following sentences by choosing the correct form from the choices in parentheses:

1. They have the (prettiest, most pretty, most prettiest) house in the neighborhood.
2. Their house is (more pretty, prettier, more prettier) than ours.
3. Of the two tigers, Sabra was the (better, best) boxer.
4. The (churches, church's) roof was damaged by the storm.
5. Bruno isn't a good soccer player, but his brother is even (worst, worse, worser).
6. Juan is (more intelligent, most intelligent) than Carl.
7. The (characters', character's) personalities are very different.

Appendix

ELEMENTS OF A SHORT STORY

SETTING	The setting of a story is the time and location in which it takes place.
CHARACTERS	Characters are the people in a story.
PLOT	The plot of a story consists of the events that happen in the story.
CONFLICT	Within the plot there is a conflict, or struggle, between characters, between a character and the environment, or within a character's mind.
THEME	A story's theme is the main idea that runs through the narrative. Sometimes, a story has several themes.

Elements of "Eleven"

SETTING	The story is set in an elementary school classroom in the United States at the present time.
CHARACTERS	Rachel, an eleven-year-old girl; Mrs. Price, her teacher; other children in Rachel's class, including Sylvia Saldívar and Phyllis Lopez
PLOT	On Rachel's eleventh birthday, Mrs. Price asks the class who owns an ugly, old sweater. When Sylvia says it belongs to Rachel, Mrs. Price believes Sylvia and insists that Rachel put it on. Rachel becomes embarrassed, starts to feel much younger than eleven, and begins to cry. After a while, Phyllis remembers that it's really her sweater. Rachel returns the sweater to Phyllis, but Mrs. Price doesn't acknowledge her mistake or apologize to Rachel, whose birthday has been ruined by the incident.
CONFLICT	Rachel knows the teacher is wrong, but she can't assert herself. She is torn between obeying an older person in a position of authority – the teacher – and asserting herself.
THEME(S)	1. children's difficulty in asserting themselves with adults 2. sensitivity of adults to children's feelings and needs 3. respect of adults for children's knowledge of the world 4. the powerful effect of teachers and school on children

Elements of _____
                    (name of story)

SETTING

CHARACTERS

PLOT

CONFLICT

THEME(S)

Vocabulary Review 1

Read each of the following sentences. Then circle the letter of the answer that gives the correct meaning for each word in **bold** print.

1. I **considered** staying home to study, but decided to go to a movie instead.
   a. decided against
   b. thought about
   c. forgot about
   d. tried

2. After running in the marathon, Jane walked **wearily** home.
   a. nervously
   b. slowly
   c. tiredly
   d. agitatedly

3. The customer **suspected** the diamonds were fake and decided not to buy them.
   a. was completely sure
   b. thought, but wasn't completely sure
   c. believed absolutely
   d. knew

4. Mary was waiting **eagerly** for her boyfriend to return from his trip.
   a. with excitement and anticipation
   b. with compassion
   c. radiantly and with anticipation
   d. alertly

5. The company's **annual** report is always published at the end of December.
   a. twice a year
   b. once every three months
   c. once a month
   d. once a year

6. That salesman is a **nuisance.** He calls every night trying to sell us his products.
   a. a bad person
   b. a ridiculous person
   c. an annoying person
   d. an unpleasant person

7. The rich woman felt **compassion** for the poor and frequently gave food and clothes to homeless people.
   a. sorry
   b. sympathy and tenderness
   c. sympathy and a desire to help
   d. concern

8. Police ordered everyone to **abandon** their homes when the river began to flood the land.
   a. leave
   b. prepare
   c. repair
   d. lock

9. Bill received so many **compliments** the first time he painted a picture that he decided to study painting seriously.
   a. interesting comments
   b. questions
   c. positive comments
   d. reactions

10. I asked someone how to get to the train station, but the directions he gave me were so **vague** that I got lost.
    a. strange
    b. unclear
    c. unusual
    d. complicated

Vocabulary Review 2

Match each vocabulary word in the left column with the best explanation on the right. Write the letter of the explanation in the space provided.

_____ 1. scared	a. say no
_____ 2. intimate	b. do what someone tells you
_____ 3. pretend	c. figure something out; judge the value of something
_____ 4. harsh	
_____ 5. diary	d. hurt
_____ 6. scowl	e. frightened
_____ 7. attic	f. hard; not easy to bend or move
_____ 8. comprehend	g. very angry
_____ 9. wounded	h. feeling satisfaction for something you have or have achieved; showing respect for yourself
_____ 10. emerge	
_____ 11. calculate	i. silly; absurd
_____ 12. proud	j. a way of behaving that has been followed for a long time
_____ 13. grateful	k. behave as if something is true even though you know it isn't
_____ 14. shiver	
_____ 15. obey	l. come out
_____ 16. stiff	m. very close
_____ 17. tradition	n. rough; cruel
_____ 18. ridiculous	o. journal
_____ 19. refuse	p. facial expression that shows anger
_____ 20. furious	q. room at the top of a house
	r. understand
	s. shake because of feeling cold
	t. thankful

Form Review

In each sentence below, choose the correct answer from the alternatives in parentheses and write it in the space provided.

1. _____ (I'm, Am I) going to visit my cousin this evening.

   _____ (Were, We're) going to go to a movie together.

2. One of Rachel's teachers _____ (do, does) not understand her

   students.

3. My sister and _____ (I, me) like our aunt so much that we

   bought gifts for our mother and _____ (she, her) on Mother's

   Day.

4. You must drive _____ (slow, slowly) through the tunnel.

5. The roses she bought smell _____ (sweet, sweetly).

6. Of the two tigers, Sabra was the _____ (better, best) boxer.

7. Our clothes _____ (needs, need) cleaning.

8. Yesterday morning the sun shone so _____ (bright, brightly)

   that it woke me at six o'clock.

9. After lunch, we _____ (washed out, washed up) the dishes.

10. I _____ (watched, was watching) television when the phone

    _____ (rang, was ringing).

11. As Anita walked _____ (in, into) the department store, she

    noticed a colorful display of sweaters _____ (on, in, into) a

    table near the entrance.

12. Jon bought Ellen _____ (a, the) gift for her birthday. He'll give

    her _____ (a, the) gift at her birthday party tomorrow.

13. This morning I'm going to have my _____ (hair, hairs) cut,

    and this afternoon I'm going to shop for _____ (furniture,

    furnitures) for my new apartment.

14. Carl _____ (send, sent) me a postcard from Spain.

15. All the _____ (guests', guests) coats were hung in the hall closet.

16. I put a pen, a pencil, and _____ (a, the) notepad in my book bag before I left home, but when I opened my bag in class, I couldn't find _____ (a, the) pen.

17. It was so hot for the marathon that the runners _____ (drank, drinks) lots of water during the race.

18. My friends and _____ (I, me) went to the movies last night. They met _____ (I, me) at my apartment, and we walked to the movie theater.

19. The boxes of cereal in the supermarket _____ (is, are) on the top shelf _____ (in, on) Aisle 3.

20. _____ (Its, It's) time to go home now.

Cause and effect One event in a story or text is often the direct result of another. In other words, one thing happens; then, as a result, a second thing happens. The first event is the cause, and the next event (or events) is the effect.

Characters The people in a story are called the characters.

Conflict Within the plot there is a conflict, or struggle, between characters, between a character and the environment, or within a character's mind.

Dialogue The characters' conversations are called dialogue.

Fable A fable is a short story with a moral, or a lesson. The characters in fables are often animals who speak and act like humans. The most famous fables were written by Aesop, a Greek slave living in the sixth century B.C. Another famous writer of fables was the seventeenth century French author La Fontaine.

First person narrator This means that the story is told in the first person by a character, often the main character, who refers to him- or herself as "I." Therefore, the reader learns what happens in the story from the perspective of the character telling it.

Foreshadowing The hints and clues that the author puts in a story to prepare you for what is going to happen are called foreshadowing.

Imagery In literature, the term imagery refers to the descriptive language that the author uses to paint a picture of the situation, characters, setting, or anything else of importance in the author's story.

Irony In literature, irony frequently occurs when there is a difference between what is expected or desired and what actually happens. For example, what a character thinks will happen to him may turn out to be the exact opposite of what actually does happen.

Plot The plot of a story consists of the events that happen in the story. The plot often has four parts: (1) the *introduction,* where the main character(s) and the situation are introduced; (2) the *complications,* or the events that happen once the situation has been introduced; (3) the *climax* of the story, or the most important event, which usually occurs near the end and brings some change; (4) the *conclusion* of the story, when the situation is resolved in some way and the story comes to an end.

Poetic justice In real life, people don't necessarily get what they deserve. However, in fiction, authors can reward or punish characters for their actions. This is called poetic justice (because it is literary and the characters get what they deserve).

Realism In literature, realism gives us a picture of life as it really is. Stories of realism deal with everyday problems that most people encounter.

Setting The setting of a story is the time and location in which it takes place.

Surprise ending A surprise ending is a sudden and unexpected ending.

Symbolism A symbol is a thing (most often a concrete object of some type) that represents an idea or a group of ideas. Symbols are often used in literary works. Examples of stories with symbolism are "The Blanket," "The Bracelet," and "The Mirror."

Theme A story's theme is the main idea that runs through the narrative. Sometimes, a story has several themes.

Irregular Verbs

Verb	Past Tense	Past Participle (use with *has, have,* and *had*)
awake	awoke, awaked	awoken, awoke
be (am, is, are)	was (were)	been
bear	bore	borne
beat	beat	beaten, beat
become	became	become
begin	began	begun
bet	bet	bet
bite	bit	bitten
blow	blew	blown
break	broke	broken
bring	brought	brought
build	built	built
burst	burst	burst
catch	caught	caught
choose	chose	chosen
cling	clung	clung
come	came	come
cost	cost	cost
creep	crept	crept
cut	cut	cut
dive	dived, dove	dived, dove
do	did	done
draw	drew	drawn
dream	dreamt, dreamed	dreamt, dreamed
drink	drank	drunk
drive	drove	driven
eat	ate	eaten
fall	fell	fallen
feel	felt	felt
fight	fought	fought
fling	flung	flung
fly	flew	flown
forget	forgot	forgotten
freeze	froze	frozen
get	got	got, gotten
give	gave	given
go	went	gone
grow	grew	grown
hang	hung	hung
hang (a person, kill)	hanged, hung	hanged, hung

hear	heard	heard
hit	hit	hit
hurt	hurt	hurt
keep	kept	kept
know	knew	known
lay	laid	laid
lead	led	led
leave	left	left
let	let	let
lie (position)	lay	lain
lose	lost	lost
make	made	made
pay	paid	paid
put	put	put
read	read (pronounced *red*)	read (pronounced *red*)
ride	rode	ridden
ring	rang	rung
rise	rose	risen
run	run	run
say	said	said
see	saw	seen
send	sent	sent
set	set	set
shake	shook	shaken
shine	shone	shone
show	showed	shown, showed
sing	sang	sung
sink	sank	sunk
sit	sat	sat
sleep	slept	slept
slide	slid	slid
speak	spoke	spoken
spring	sprang	sprung
steal	stole	stolen
swear	swore	sworn
swim	swam	swum
swing	swung	swung
take	took	taken
teach	taught	taught
tear	tore	torn
tell	told	told
think	thought	thought
throw	threw	thrown
wake	woke	woken
wear	wore	worn
win	won	won
write	wrote	written

Past Tense and Participle Forms of Regular Verbs

One-Syllable Verbs in Past Tense and Participle Forms

1. **One-syllable verbs that end in *e***   To form the past tense and past participle, drop the final *e* and add *-ed*. To form the present participle, drop the final *e* and add *-ing*. Here are some examples:

PRESENT	PAST/PAST PARTICIPLE	PRESENT PARTICIPLE
care	cared	caring
scare	scared	scaring
hope	hoped	hoping
date	dated	dating

2. **One-syllable verbs that end in a vowel preceded by a consonant**   To form the past tense and past participle, double the final consonant and add *-ed*. To form the present participle, double the final consonant and add *-ing*. Here are some examples:

PRESENT	PAST/PAST PARTICIPLE	PRESENT PARTICIPLE
stop	stopped	stopping
hop	hopped	hopping
plan	planned	planning
sob	sobbed	sobbing

3. **One-syllable verbs that end in two consonants**   To form the past tense and past participle, add *-ed*. To form the present participle, add *-ing*. Here are some examples:

PRESENT	PAST/PAST PARTICIPLE	PRESENT PARTICIPLE
start	started	starting
walk	walked	walking
fold	folded	folding
warn	warned	warning

4. **One-syllable verbs that end in a consonant preceded by two vowels** To form the past tense and past participle, add *-ed*. To form the present participle, add *-ing*. Here are some examples:

PRESENT	PAST/PAST PARTICIPLE	PRESENT PARTICIPLE
look	looked	looking
cook	cooked	cooking
wait	waited	waiting
stain	stained	staining

Two-Syllable Verbs in Past Tense and Participle Forms

1. **Two-syllable verbs with stress on the first syllable** (If you're not sure which syllable is stressed, check your dictionary.) To form the past tense and past participle, add *-ed*. To form the present participle, add *-ing*. Here are some examples:

PRESENT	PAST/PAST PARTICIPLE	PRESENT PARTICIPLE
happen	happened	happening
offer	offered	offering
listen	listened	listening
open	opened	opening

2. **Two-syllable verbs with stress on the second syllable** (If you're not sure which syllable is stressed, check your dictionary.) To form the past tense or past participle, double the final consonant and add *-ed*. To form the present participle, double the final consonant and add *-ing*. Here are some examples:

PRESENT	PAST/PAST PARTICIPLE	PRESENT PARTICIPLE
occur	occurred	occurring
prefer	preferred	preferring
control	controlled	controlling
admit	admitted	admitting

3. **Two-syllable verbs that end in *ss* or *st*** To form the past tense and past participle, add *-ed*. (Do not double the final consonant, even though the second syllable is stressed.) To form the present participle, add *-ing*. (Do not double the final consonant, even though the second syllable is stressed.) Here are some examples:

PRESENT	PAST/PAST PARTICIPLE	PRESENT PARTICIPLE
confess	confessed	confessing
depress	depressed	depressing
insist	insisted	insisting
consist	consisted	consisting

4. **Two-syllable verbs that end in a consonant preceded by two vowels** To form the past tense and past participle, add *-ed*. (Do not double the final consonant, even though the second syllable is stressed.) To form the present participle, add *-ing*. (Do not double the final consonant, even though the second syllable is stressed.) Here are some examples:

PRESENT	PAST/PAST PARTICIPLE	PRESENT PARTICIPLE
conceal	concealed	concealing
reveal	revealed	revealed
repeat	repeated	repeating
complain	complained	complaining

Verbs Ending in y *in the Past Tense and Participle Forms*

1. **Verbs ending in *y* in which *y* is preceded by a consonant** To form the past tense and past participle, change *y* to *i* and add *-ed*. To form the present participle, keep the *y* and add *-ing*. Here are some examples:

PRESENT	PAST/PAST PARTICIPLE	PRESENT PARTICIPLE
cry	cried	crying
try	tried	trying
reply	replied	replying
deny	denied	denying

2. **Verbs ending in _y_ in which _y_ is preceded by a vowel**   To form the past tense and past participle, keep the _y_ and add _-ed_. To form the present participle, keep the _y_ and add _-ing_. Here are some examples:

PRESENT	PAST/PAST PARTICIPLE	PRESENT PARTICIPLE
pray	prayed	praying
employ	employed	employing
play	played	playing
destroy	destroyed	destroying

Plural Forms of Nouns

Plural Form of Nouns Ending in y Preceded by a Consonant

To form the plural, change the _y_ to _i_ and add _-es_. Here are some examples:

SINGULAR	PLURAL
diary	diaries
baby	babies
city	cities
activity	activities

Plural Form of Nouns Ending in y Preceded by a Vowel

To form the plural, keep the _y_ and add _-s_. Here are some examples:

SINGULAR	PLURAL
key	keys
attorney	attorneys
alley	alleys
toy	toys

Plural Form of Nouns Ending in o

1. **Plural form of nouns ending in *o* preceded by a vowel**   To form the plural, simply add *-s*. Here are some examples:

SINGULAR	PLURAL
radio	radios
patio	patios
studio	studios
zoo	zoos

2. **Plural form of nouns ending in *o* preceded by a consonant**   To form the plural, add *-es*. Here are some examples:

SINGULAR	PLURAL
hero	heroes
echo	echoes
tomato	tomatoes
potato	potatoes

3. **Plural form of nouns ending in *o* that are musical terms**   To form the plural, add *-s* regardless of whether the final *o* is preceded by a vowel or consonant. Here are some examples:

SINGULAR	PLURAL
soprano	sopranos
piano	pianos
trio	trios
solo	solos

ie *and* ei *Words*

To remember which comes first, the *i* or the *e*, it may be helpful to learn this rhyme:

Put *i* before *e*
Except after *c*
Or when sounded like *a*
As in *neighbor* and *weigh*

Here are some examples:

ie WORDS	*ei* WORDS
believe	deceive
relief	receive
niece	receipt
brief	conceit
friend	freight (an *a* sound)
piece	vein (an *a* sound)
thief	their (an *a* sound)
grief	eight (an *a* sound)

Some words that don't follow these patterns are *either, neither, height, foreign, weird, science,* and *ancient.*

Acknowledgments

Sandra Cisneros, "Eleven," from *Woman Hollering Creek and Other Stories*. Random House, Inc., New York, 1991. Copyright © 1991 by Sandra Cisneros. Reprinted by permission of Susan Bergholtz Literary Services, New York. All rights reserved.

Floyd Dell, "The Blanket," from *Collier's*, October 16, 1926. Reprinted with permission of the Estate of Floyd Dell.

Yoshiko Uchida, "The Bracelet," from *The Scribner Anthology for Young People*, edited by Annie Diven. Copyright © 1976 by Yoshiko Uchida. Reprinted by permission of Antheum Books for Young Readers, an imprint of Simon & Schuster Children's Publishing Division.

Quentin Reynolds, "A Secret for Two." Copyright © 1936, Cromwell-Collier Publishing Co. Reprinted by permission of the Estate of Quentin Reynolds.

Jane Yolen, "Johanna." Copyright © 1983 by Jane Yolen. Published in *Tales of Wonder*, published by Schocken Books (Random House). Reprinted by permission of Curtis Brown, Ltd.

O. Henry, "Two Thanksgiving Day Gentlemen" (adaptation). From "Two Thanksgiving Day Gentlemen" in *The Complete Works of O. Henry* published by Garden City Books, a division of Bantam Doubleday Dell, Inc.

Isaac Asimov, "The Fun They Had," from *Earth Is Room Enough* by Isaac Asimov, copyright © 1957 by Isaac Asimov. Used by permission of Doubleday, a division of Random House, Inc.

Judith Kay, *"The Mirror."* Copyright © 1996 by Judith Kay. Reprinted by permission of the author.

William Saroyan, "You Go Your Way, I'll Go Mine," from *The Human Comedy*, copyright © 1943 by William Saroyan. Reprinted by permission of Harcourt, Inc. and the Trustees of Leland Stanford Junior University.

Corey Ford, "Snake Dance." Reprinted courtesy of the Trustees of Dartmouth College.

Gwendolyn Brooks, "Home," a chapter from the novel *Maud Martha* by Gwendolyn Brooks, copyright © 1991, published by Third World Press, Chicago, 1991.

Zona Gale, "The Woman." Reprinted with permission of Leslyn Breese Keie.

James Thurber, "The Tigress and Her Mate," from *Further Fables for Our Time*, copyright © 1956 by James Thurber. Copyright © renewed 1984 by Rosemary A. Thurber. Reprinted by arrangement with Rosemary A. Thurber and The Barbara Hogeson Agency. All rights reserved.

Kate Chopin, "The Kiss." Reprinted by permission of Louisiana State University Press from *The Complete Works of Kate Chopin*, by Kate Chopin. Copyright © 1997 by Louisiana State University Press.

Index